# THE PARADISE OF BOMBS

# The Paradise of

# B·O·M·B·S

## SCOTT RUSSELL SANDERS

**BEACON PRESS**

BOSTON

Beacon Press
25 Beacon Street
Boston, Massachusetts 02108-2892
www.beacon.org

Beacon Press books
are published under the auspices of
the Unitarian Universalist Association of Congregations.

Published in arrangement with the University of Georgia Press

First digital-print edition 2001

*Library of Congress Cataloging-in-Publication Data*
Sanders, Scott R. (Scott Russell), 1945–
The paradise of bombs / Scott Russell Sanders.
p.    cm.
ISBN 0-8070-6343-6
I. Title.
PS3569.A5137P36    1993
814'.54—dc20    92-30536

Winner of the Associated Writing Programs
Award for Creative Nonfiction

*For George and Barbara Morgan,*
*guides to the world's inwardness*

But ask now the beasts, and they shall teach thee;
And the birds of the air, and they shall tell thee:
Or speak to the earth, and it shall teach thee.
Job 12: 7–8

Could a greater miracle take place than for us to look
through each other's eyes for an instant?
Henry David Thoreau

# CONTENTS

# ACKNOWLEDGMENTS

I am especially grateful to Robley Wilson, Jr., editor of *The North American Review,* for giving a home to so many of these essays, including earlier versions of "At Play in the Paradise of Bombs," "Cloud Crossing," "Coming from the Country," "Death Games" (under the title "Bang, Bang, You're Dead"), "Digging Limestone," "Doing Time in the Thirteenth Chair," "The Inheritance of Tools," "In Stone Country," and "Listening to Owls." "Feasting on Mountains" originally appeared in *Inprint,* and "The Men We Carry in Our Minds" in *Milkweed Chronicle.*

# INTRODUCTION

The pieces gathered in this book are essays, by which I mean they are experiments in making sense of things, and they are personal, by which I mean the voice speaking is the nearest I can come to my own voice. For me the writing of a personal essay is like finding my way through a forest without being quite sure what game I am chasing, what landmark I am seeking. I sniff down one path until some heady smell tugs me in a new direction, and then off I go, dodging and circling, lured on by the calls of unfamiliar birds, puzzled by the tracks of strange beasts, leaping from stone to stone across rivers, barking up one tree after another. The pleasure in writing an essay—and, when the writing is any good, the pleasure in reading it—comes from this dodging and leaping, this movement of the mind.

It must not be idle movement, however, if the essay is to hold up; it must yield a pattern, draw a map of experience, be driven by deep concerns. The surface of a river is alive with lights and reflections, the breaking of foam over rocks, but underneath that dazzle it is going somewhere. We should expect as much from an essay: the shimmer and play of mind on the surface and in the depths a strong current.

Most of the fashions in fiction of the past twenty years have led away from candor—toward irony, satire, artsy jokes, close-lipped coyness, anything but a serious, direct statement of what the author thinks and feels. If you hide behind enough screens, no one will ever hold you to an opinion or demand from you a coherent vision or take you for a charlatan. The essay appeals to me because it is not hedged round by these literary inhibitions. You may speak without disguise of what moves and worries and excites you. If the words you put down are foolish, then at least everyone knows who the fool is.

Reading back through this book, I find myself brooding in essay after essay on the origins of violence, especially that collective madness we call war; on the ways we inhabit the land; on our fellowship with animals; on the use of hands; on the tangled legacy of maleness; on the mysterious gravitation of love. But such an abstract listing of themes is misleading, for the essays themselves deal only in the concrete and particular. They are narratives; they speak about the world in stories, in terms of human actions and speech and the tangible world we inhabit. I have written of things that haunt me—owls and hammers and guns and deer. I have described the quarrying of limestone and the building of rockets and the coddling of babies. I have told about climbing mountains and serving on a jury; about growing up on a military base and working on farms, fixing machines and breaking hearts; about the terror of taxis, the mystery of menus, the intricate dance of nature.

Some years ago I lived for a spell in Louisiana, near the Gulf of Mexico. After hurricanes, as I drove through the rice paddies that stretched flat to the edge of the world, I would find refrigerators and bathtubs scattered over the fields where the high waters had flung them. Just so, the subjects of these essays have lodged in my mind. They are what I find, what I cannot ignore, the images and memories that gleam in the landscape of consciousness, like those bathtubs and refrigerators gleaming white against the dark green of rice paddies. Wherever they come from, they are bound together by the flood that lifted and carried them and exposed them to view.

By dealing with matters that move and trouble me, these essays are personal without being, except incidentally, autobiographical. I write of my own life only when it seems to have a larger bearing on the lives of others. Thus I tell what it was like to grow up in a military arsenal because I am convinced we all now live in an armed camp. I tell of my father's death because it focused for me lessons about the virtue and fragility of human skill. I tell of puzzling over what it means to be a "man" because the spectacle of women waking to their own full powers has pushed—or should have pushed—all men to such puzzling. I tell of sitting as a juror in a drug trial because the experience made me realize how we are bound to err in our judgments of one another. Mostly, however, I write in a personal voice about the impersonal, the not-me, for the world is a larger and more interesting place than my ego. Put another way, these essays are my effort at remembering where we truly live—not inside a skull, a house, a town or nation, not inside any human creation at all, but in *the* creation.

The dance of nature has been on people's minds more than usual lately, with the ballyhooed return of Halley's Comet. Surely it is a greater marvel, I tell myself, for my heart to beat sixty times a minute than for a ball of ice to swing around the sun every seventy-six years. Still, whenever I look at the sky these nights, I find my skeptical heart kicking up into a faster pace. A few cold evenings ago, my wife, daughter, son, and I walked to the park near our home to look for Mr. Halley's wonder. The newspaper had announced that an astronomer would be there to help people find the comet, so a crowd had gathered. The four of us huddled together among strangers in the knifing cold darkness and searched the sky with binoculars. We had only the vaguest notion where to look. I calculated that my son and daughter, at eight and twelve years old, would have a chance of seeing the comet on its next visit, in 2062. I knew this would be my only season.

"Does anyone need help?" a voice called from the crowd.

The Sanders family gave a shout. Presently a man loomed out

of the darkness, his face a disk of shadow under a parka hood, and he gave us directions for looking. His words drew imagined lines on the sky for us, beginning with Jupiter down near the western horizon, swinging up to the Great Square in Pegasus, back to the Y-shaped Water Jar in Aquarius, and so on star by star until our gaze reached a tiny blur of light. "That's Halley's Comet," said the astronomer, and he drifted away to help other searchers.

We took our turns at the binoculars, mother and daughter, father and son.

"*That's* the comet?" said my daughter when her turn came. "That little smudge? That's *all*?"

"Where is it?" my son cried. "I can't see it. Everything's fuzzy."

I pointed, aimed the binoculars for him, but still he could not find the firefly in the glitter of stars. He was trembling. I squatted down and took his face in my hands to guide his looking and whispered directions in his ear.

"Do you see it now?" My breath cast a cloud about our heads.

"I don't know," he said, his voice raw with frustration, "I can't tell, it's all a jumble. There's too many lights. What if I *miss* it?"

I felt like weeping, there in the night among strangers, holding my son's face and murmuring in his ear, because I could not see through his eyes, he could not see through mine, and all I had to offer were a few words to draw lines on the darkness. Since it was all I knew how to do, I kept murmuring, stringing words into sentences, sentences into galaxies and constellations.

At length he murmured, "I think I see it. Yes, there it is. I see what you're saying."

But whether he saw the comet, or only my words sketched over the darkness, I do not know.

S.R.S.

Bloomington, Indiana
January 1986

# AT PLAY
# IN THE PARADISE OF BOMBS

**T**wice a man's height and topped by strands of barbed wire, a chain-link fence stretched for miles along the highway leading up to the main gate of the Arsenal. Beside the gate were tanks, hulking dinosaurs of steel, one on each side, their long muzzles slanting down to catch trespassers in a cross-fire. A soldier emerged from the gatehouse, gun on hip, silvered sunglasses blanking his eyes.

My father stopped our car. He leaned out the window and handed the guard some papers which my mother had been nervously clutching.

"With that license plate, I had you pegged for visitors," said the guard. "But I see you've come to stay."

His flat voice ricocheted against the rolled-up windows of the back seat where I huddled beside my sister. I hid my face in the upholstery, to erase the barbed wire and tanks and mirror-eyed soldier, and tried to wind myself into a ball as tight as the fist of fear in my stomach. By and by, our car eased forward into the Arsenal, the paradise of bombs.

This was in April of 1951, in Ohio. We had driven north from Tennessee, where spring had already burst the buds of trees and cracked the flowers open. Up here on the hem of Lake Erie the earth was bleak with snow. I had been told about northern winters, but in the red clay country south of Memphis I had seen only occasional flurries, harmless as confetti, never this smother-

1

ing quilt of white. My mother had been crying since Kentucky. Sight of the Arsenal's fences and guard shacks looming out of the snow brought her misery to the boil. "It's like a concentration camp," she whispered to my father. I had no idea what she meant. I was not quite six, born two months after the gutting of Hiroshima and Nagasaki. My birth sign was the mushroom cloud. "It looks exactly like those pictures of the German camps," she lamented. Back in Tennessee, the strangers who had bought our farm were clipping bouquets from her garden. Those strangers had inherited everything—the barn and jittery cow, the billy goat fond of cornsilks, the crops of beans and potatoes already planted, the creek bottom cleared of locust trees, the drawling voices of neighbors, the smell of cotton dust.

My father had worked through the Second World War at a munitions plant near his hometown in Mississippi. Now his company, hired by the Pentagon to run this Ohio Arsenal, was moving him north to supervise the production lines where artillery shells and land mines and bombs were loaded with explosives. Later I would hear stories about those loadlines. The concrete floors were so saturated with TNT that any chance spark would set off a quake. The workers used tools of brass to guard against sparks, but every now and again a careless chump would drop a pocket knife or shell casing, and lose a leg. Once a forklift dumped a pallet of barrels and blew out an entire factory wall, along with three munitions loaders.

In 1951 I was too young to realize that what had brought on all this bustle in our lives was the war in Korea; too green to notice which way the political winds were blowing. Asia was absorbing bullets and bombs as quickly as the Arsenal could ship them. At successive news conferences, President Truman meditated aloud on whether or not to spill *the* Bomb—the sip of planetary hemlock—over China. Senator McCarthy was denouncing Reds from every available podium, pinning a single handy label on all

2

the bugbears of the nation. Congress had recently passed bills designed to hamstring unions and slam the doors of America in the faces of immigrants. The Soviet Union had detonated its own atomic weapons, and the search was on for the culprits who had sold our secret. How else but through treachery could such a benighted nation ever have built such a clever bomb? In the very month of our move to the Arsenal, Julius and Ethel Rosenberg were sentenced to death. Too late, J. Robert Oppenheimer was voicing second thoughts about the weapon he had helped build. In an effort to preserve our lead in the race toward oblivion, our scientists were perfecting the hydrogen bomb.

We rolled to our new home in the Arsenal over the impossible snow, between parking lots filled with armored troop carriers, jeeps, strafing helicopters, wheeled howitzers, bulldozers, Sherman tanks, all the brawny machines of war. On the front porch of our Memphis home I had read GI Joe comic books, and so I knew the names and shapes of these death-dealing engines. In the gaudy cartoons the soldiers had seemed like two-legged chunks of pure glory, muttering speeches between bursts on their machine guns, clenching the pins of grenades between their dazzling teeth. Their weapons had seemed like tackle worthy of gods. But as we drove between those parking lots crowded with real tanks, past guard houses manned by actual soldiers, a needle of dread pierced my brain.

Thirty years later the needle is still there, and is festering. I realize now that in moving from a scrape-dirt farm in Tennessee to a munitions factory in Ohio I had leaped overnight from the nineteenth century into the heart of the twentieth. I had landed in a place that concentrates the truth about our condition more potently than any metropolis or suburb. If, one hundred years from now, there are still human beings capable of thinking about the past, and if they turn their sights on our own time, what they will see through the cross hairs of memory will be a place very

3

like the Arsenal, a fenced wilderness devoted to the building and harboring of the instruments of death.

Our house was one of twenty white frame boxes arrayed in a circle about a swatch of lawn. Originally built for the high-ranking military brass, some of these government quarters now also held civilians—the doctors assigned to the base hospital, the engineers who carried slide-rules dangling from their belts, the accountants and supervisors, the managerial honchos. In our children's argot, this hoop of houses became the Circle, the beginning and ending point of all our journeys. Like campers drawn up around a fire, like wagons wound into a fearful ring, the houses faced inward on the Circle, as if to reassure the occupants, for immediately outside that tamed hoop the forest began, a tangled, beast-haunted woods stretching for miles in every direction.

Through our front door I looked out on mowed grass, flower boxes, parked cars, the curves of concrete, the wink of windows. From the back door I saw only trees, bare dark bones thrust up from the snow in that first April, snarled green shadows in all the following summers. Not many nights after we had settled in, I glimpsed a white-tailed deer lurking along the edge of that woods out back, the first of thousands I would see over the years. The Arsenal was a sanctuary for deer, I soon learned, and also for beaver, fox, turkey, geese, every manner of beast smaller than wolves and bears. Protected by that chain-link fence, which kept out hunters and woodcutters as well as spies, the animals had multiplied to very nearly their ancient numbers, and the trees grew thick and old until they died with their roots on. So throughout my childhood I had a choice of where to play—inside the charmed Circle or outside in the wild thickets.

Viewed on a map against Ohio's bulldozed land, the Arsenal was only a tiny patch of green, about thirty square miles; some of it had been pasture as recently as ten years earlier, when the government bought the land. It was broken up by airstrips and bunkers and munitions depots; guards cruised its perimeter and bored through its heart twenty-four hours a day. But to my young eyes it seemed like an unbounded wilderness. The biggest parcel of land for the Arsenal had belonged to a U.S. senator, who—in the selfless tradition of public servants—grew stinking rich from the sale. The rest was purchased from farmers, some of them descendants of the hardbitten New England folks who had settled that corner of Ohio, most of them reluctant to move. One of the old-timers refused to budge from his house until the wrecking crew arrived, and then he slung himself from a noose tied to a rafter in his barn. By the time I came along to investigate, all that remained of his place was the crumbling silo; but I found it easy to imagine him strung up there, roped to his roof-beam, riding his ship as it went down. Every other year or so, the older children would string a scarecrow from a rafter in one of the few surviving barns, and then lead the younger children in for a grisly look. I only fell for the trick once, but the image of that dangling husk is burned into my mind.

Rambling through the Arsenal's twenty-one thousand acres, at first in the safe back seats of our parents' cars, then on bicycles over the gravel roads, and later on foot through the backcountry, we children searched out the ruins of those abandoned farms. Usually the buildings had been torn down and carted away, and all that remained were the cellar holes half-filled with rubble, the skewed limestone foundations, the stubborn flowers. What used to be lawns were grown up in sumac, maple, blackberry. The rare concrete walks and driveways were shattered, sown to ferns. Moss grew in the chiseled names of the dead on headstones in backyard cemeteries. We could spy a house site in the spring by the blaze of jonquils, the blue fountain of lilacs, the forsythia and starry columbine; in the summer by roses; in the fall by the glow of mums and zinnias. Asparagus and rhubarb kept pushing up through the meadows. The blasted orchards kept squeezing out plums and knotty apples and bee-thick pears. From the cellar

5

holes wild grapevines twisted up to ensnarl the shade trees. In the ruins we discovered marbles, bottles, the bone handles of knives, the rusty heads of hammers, and the tips of plows. And we dug up keys by the fistful, keys of brass and black iron, skeleton keys to ghostly doors. We gathered the fruits of other people's planting, staggering home with armfuls of flowers, sprays of pussywillow and bittersweet, baskets of berries, our faces sticky with juice.

Even where the army's poisons had been dumped, nature did not give up. In a remote corner of the Arsenal, on land which had been used as a Boy Scout camp before the war, the ground was so filthy with the discarded makings of bombs that not even guards would go there. But we children went, lured on by the scarlet warning signs. DANGER. RESTRICTED AREA. The skull-and-crossbones aroused in us dreams of pirates. We found the log huts overgrown with vines, the swimming lake a bog of algae and cattails, the stone walls scattered by the heave of frost. The only scrap of metal we discovered was a bell, its clapper rusted solid to the rim. In my bone marrow I carry traces of the poison from that graveyard of bombs, as we all carry a smidgen of radioactivity from every atomic blast. Perhaps at this very moment one of those alien molecules, like a grain of sand in an oyster, is irritating some cell in my body, or in your body, to fashion a pearl of cancer.

Poking about in the ruins of camp and farms, I felt a wrestle of emotions, half sick with loss, half exultant over the return of forest. It was terrifying and at the same time comforting to see how quickly the green wave lapped over the human remains, scouring away the bold marks of occupation. The displaced farmers, gone only a decade, had left scarcely more trace than the ancient Indians who had heaped up burial mounds in this territory. We hunted for Indian treasure, too, digging in every suspicious hillock until our arms ached. We turned up shards of pottery, iridescent shells, fiery bits of flint; but never any bones. The best arrow points and ax-heads we invariably discovered not by looking, but by chance, when jumping over a creek or scratching in the dirt with a bare incurious toe. This was my first lesson in the Zen of seeing, seeing by not-looking.

With or without looking, we constantly stumbled across the more common variety of mound in the Arsenal, the hump-backed bunkers where munitions were stored. Implausibly enough, they were called igloos. There were rows and rows of them, strung out along rail beds like lethal beads. Over the concrete vaults grass had been planted, so that from the air, glimpsed by enemy bombers, they would look like undulating hills. Sheep kept them mowed. The signs surrounding the igloos were larger and more strident than those warning us to keep away from the waste dumps. These we respected, for we feared that even a heavy footfall on the grassy roof of a bunker might set it off. Three or four had blown up over the years, from clumsy handling or the quirk of chemicals. Once a jet trainer crashed into a field of them and skidded far enough to trigger a pair. These numbers multiplied in our minds, until we imagined the igloos popping like corn. No, no, they were set far enough apart to avoid a chain reaction if one should explode, my father assured me. But in my reckoning the munitions bunkers were vaults of annihilation. I stubbornly believed that one day they all would blow, touched off by lightning, maybe, or by an enemy agent. Whenever I stole past those fields of bunkers or whenever they drifted like a flotilla of green hump-backed whales through my dreams, I imagined fire leaping from one to another, the spark flying outward to consume the whole creation. This poison I also carry in my bones, this conviction that we build our lives in mine fields. Long before I learned what new sort of bombs had devoured Hiroshima and Nagasaki, I knew from creeping among those igloos full of old-fashioned explosives that, on any given day, someone else's reckless step might consume us all.

Of course we played constantly at war. How could we avoid it? At the five-and-dime we bought plastic soldiers, their fists molded

7

permanently around machine guns and grenades, their faces frozen into expressions of bravery or bloodlust. They were all men, all except the weaponless nurse who stood with uplifted lantern to inspect the wounded; and those of us who toyed at this mayhem were all boys. In the unused garden plot out back of the Circle, we excavated trenches and foxholes, embedded cannons inside rings of pebbles, heaped dirt into mounds to simulate ammo bunkers. Our miniature tanks left treadmarks in the dust exactly like those cut into the blacktop roads by real tanks. Running miniature trucks, our throats caught the exact groan of the diesel convoys that hauled army reservists past our door every summer weekend. When we grew tired of our Lilliputian battles, we took up weapons in our own hands. Any stick would do for a gun, any rock for a bomb. At the drugstore we bought war comics and on wet afternoons we studied war movies on television to instruct us in the plots for our games. No one ever chose to play the roles of Japs or Nazis or Commies, and so the hateful labels were hung on the smallest or shabbiest kids. For the better part of my first three years in the Arsenal I was a villain, consigned to the Yellow Peril or the Red Plague. Like many of the runts, even wearing the guise of a bad guy I refused to go down, protesting every lethal shot from the good guys. If all the kids eligible to serve as enemies quit the game, the Americans just blasted away at invisible foes, GI's against the universe.

Whenever we cared to we could glance up from our play in the garden battlefield and see the dish of a radar antenna spinning silently beyond the next ridge. We knew it scoured the sky for enemy bombers and, later, missiles. The air was filled with electronic threats. Every mile or so along the roads there were spiky transmitters, like six-foot-tall models of the Empire State Building, to magnify and boom along radio messages between security headquarters and the cruising guards. Imagining dire secrets whispered in code, I keened my ears to catch these broadcasts, as if by one particular resonance of brain cells I might snare the voices inside my skull. What I eventually heard, over a shortwave radio owned by one of the older boys, were guards jawing about lunch, muttering about the weather, about wives or bills or bowling, swearing aimlessly, or counting deer.

Our favorite family outing on the long summer evenings, after supper, after the washing of dishes, was to drive the gravel roads of the Arsenal and count deer. We would surprise them in clearings, a pair or a dozen, grass drooping from their narrow muzzles, jaws working. They would lift their delicate heads and gaze at us with slick dark eyes, some of the bucks hefting intricate antlers, the fresh does thick-uddered, the fawns still dappled. If the herd was large enough to make counting tricky, my father would stop the car. And if we kept very still, the deer, after studying us awhile, would go back to their grazing. But any slight twitch, a throat cleared or the squeak of a window crank, would startle them. First one white tail would jerk up, then another and another, the tawny bodies wheeling, legs flashing, and the deer would vanish like smoke. Some nights we counted over three hundred.

There were so many deer that in bad winters the managers of the Arsenal ordered the dumping of hay on the snow to keep the herds from starving. When my father had charge of this chore, I rode atop the truckload of bales, watching the tire slices trail away behind us in the frozen crust. Still the weak went hungry. Sledding, we would find their withered carcasses beside the gnawed stems of elderberry bushes. A few generations earlier, wolves and mountain lions would have helped out the snow, culling the slow-of-foot. But since the only predators left were two-legged ones, men took on the task of thinning the herds, and naturally they culled out the strongest, the heavy-antlered bucks, the meaty does. Early each winter the game officials would guess how many deer ought to be killed, and would sell that many hunting tags. Most of the licenses went to men who worked on the Arsenal, the carpenters and munitions loaders and firemen.

But a quantity would always be reserved for visiting military brass.

They rolled into the Arsenal in chauffeured sedans or swooped down in star-spangled planes, these generals and colonels. Their hunting clothes smelled of moth balls. Their shotguns glistened with oil. Jeeps driven by orderlies delivered them to the brushwood blinds, where they slouched on canvas chairs and slugged whiskey to keep warm, waiting for the deer to run by. The deer always ran obligingly by, because men and boys hired from nearby towns would have been out since dawn beating the bushes, scaring up a herd and driving it down the ravine past the hidden generals, who pumped lead into the torrent of flesh.

Each deer season of my childhood I heard about this hunt. It swelled in my imagination to the scale of myth, outstripped in glory the remote battles of the last war, seemed more grand even than the bloody feuds between frontiersmen and Indians. I itched to go along, cradling my own shotgun, but my father said no, not until the winter after my thirteenth birthday. If I can't carry a gun, I begged, let me watch the hunt with empty hands. And so, the year I turned eleven he let me join the beaters, who would be herding deer for a party of shooters from the Pentagon.

A freezing rain the night before had turned the world to glass. As we fanned out over the brittle snow, our bootsteps sounded like the shattering of windows. We soon found our deer, lurking where they had to be, in the frozen field where hay had been dumped. Casting about them our net of bodies, we left open only the path that led to the ravine where the officers waited. With a clap of hands we set them scurrying, the white tails like an avalanche, black hoofs punching the snow, lank hams kicking skyward. Not long after, we heard the crackle of shotguns. When the shooting was safely over, I hurried up to inspect the kills. The deer lay with legs crumpled beneath their bellies or jutting stiffly out, heads askew, tongues dangling like handles of leather. The wounded ones had stumbled away, trailing behind them ropes of

10

blood; my father and the other seasoned hunters had run after to finish them off. The generals were tramping about in the red snow, noisily claiming their trophies, pinning tags on the ear of each downed beast. The local men gutted the deer. They heaped the steaming entrails on the snow and tied ropes through the tendons of each hind leg and dragged them to the waiting jeeps. I watched it all to the end that once, rubbed my face in it, and never again asked to work as a beater, or to watch the grown men shoot, or to hunt.

With the money I was paid for herding deer, I bought the fixings for rocket fuel. That was the next stage in our playing at war, the launching of miniature missiles. We started by wrapping tinfoil around the heads of kitchen matches, graduated to aluminum pipes crammed with gunpowder, and then to machined tubes that burned zinc or magnesium. On the walls of our bedrooms we tacked photos of real rockets, the V-2 and Viking; the homely Snark, Hound Dog, Bullpup, Honest John, Little John, Mighty Mouse, Davy Crockett; and the beauties with godly names—Atlas, Titan, Jupiter, Juno, Nike-Hercules—the pantheon of power. By then I knew what rode in the nose cones, I knew what sort of bombs had exploded in Japan two months before my birth, I even knew, from reading physics books, how we had snared those fierce bits of sun. But I grasped these awesome facts in the same numb way I grasped the definition of infinity. I carried the knowledge in me like an ungerminated seed.

There was a rumor among the children that atomic bombs were stored in the Arsenal. The adults denied it, as they denied our belief that ghosts of Indians haunted the burial mounds or that shades of strung-up farmers paced in the haylofts of barns, as they dismissed all our bogies. We went searching anyway. Wasting no time among the igloos, which were too obvious, too vulnerable, we searched instead in the boondocks for secret vaults that we felt certain would be surrounded by deadly electronics and would be perfect in their camouflage. Traipsing along railway spurs, following every set of wheeltracks, we eventually came to a fenced compound that satisfied all our suspicions. Through the gridwork of wire and above the earthen ramparts we could see the gray concrete skulls of bunkers. We felt certain that the eggs of annihilation had been laid in those vaults, but none of us dared climb the fence to investigate. It was as if, having sought out the lair of a god, we could not bring ourselves to approach the throne.

In our searches for the Bomb we happened across a good many other spots we were not supposed to see—dumps and man-made deserts, ponds once used for hatching fish and now smothered in oil, machine guns rusting in weeds, clicking signal boxes. But the most alluring discovery of all was the graveyard of bombers. This was a field crammed with the ratty hulks of World War II Flying Fortresses, their crumpled green skins painted with enigmatic numbers and symbols, their wings twisted, propellers shattered, cockpits open to the rain. In one of them we found a pair of mannequins rigged up in flight gear, complete with helmets, wires running from every joint in their artificial bodies. What tests they had been used for in these crashed planes we had no way of guessing; we borrowed their gear and propped them in back to serve as navigators and bombardiers. Most of the instruments had been salvaged, but enough remained for us to climb into the cockpits and fly imaginary bombing runs. Sitting where actual pilots had sat, clutching the butterfly wings of a steering wheel, gazing out through a cracked windshield, we rained fire and fury on the cities of the world. Not even the sight of the deer's guts steaming on the red snow had yet given me an inkling of how real streets would look beneath our storm of bombs. I was drunk on the fancied splendor of riding those metal leviathans, making them dance by a touch of my fingers. At the age when Samuel Clemens sat on the bank of the Mississippi River smitten by the power of steamboats, I watched rockets sputter on their firing stand, I sat in the gutted cockpits of old bombers, hungry to pilot sky ships.

The sky over the Arsenal was sliced by plenty of routine ships, the screaming fighters, droning trainers, groaning transports, percussive helicopters; but what caught the attention of the children were the rare, rumored visitations of flying saucers. To judge by reports in the newspaper and on television, UFOs were sniffing about here and there all over the earth. We studied the night sky hopefully, fearfully, but every promising light we spied turned into a commonplace aircraft. I was beginning to think the aliens had declared the Arsenal off-limits. But then a neighbor woman, who sometimes looked after my sister and me in the afternoons, told us she had ridden more than once in a flying saucer that used to come fetch her in the wee hours from the parking lot behind the Bachelor Officers' Quarters. Mrs. K. was about fifty when we knew her, a stunted woman who gave the impression of being too large for her body, as if at birth she had been wrapped in invisible cords which were beginning to give way; she had a pinched face and watery eyes, a mousy book-keeper for a husband, and no children. She was fastidious about her house, where the oak floors gleamed with wax, bathrooms glittered like jeweled chambers, and fragile knickknacks balanced on shelves of glass. When my mother dropped us by her place for an afternoon's stay, we crept about in terror of sullying or break-ing something. In all her house there was nothing for children to play with except, stashed away in the bottom drawer of her desk, a dogeared pack of cards, a pair of dice, and a miniature roulette wheel. Soon tiring of these toys, my sister and I sat on the waxed floor and wheedled her into talking. At first she would maunder on about the life she had led on military bases around the world, the bridge parties and sewing circles; but eventually her eyes would begin to water and her teeth to chatter and she would launch into the history of her abduction by the aliens.

"They're not at all like devils," she insisted, "but more like angels, with translucent skin that glows almost as if there were lights inside their bodies." And their ship bore no resemblance to saucers, she claimed. It was more like a diamond as large as a house, all the colors of the rainbow streaming through the facets. The angelic creatures stopped her in the parking lot during one of her stargazing walks, spoke gentle English inside her head, took her on board their craft, and put her to sleep. When she awoke she was lying naked, surrounded by a ring of princely aliens, and the landscape visible through the diamond walls of the ship was the vague purple of wisteria blossoms. "They weren't the least bit crude or nasty," she said, the words coming so fast they were jamming together in her throat, "no, no, they examined me like the most polite of doctors, because all they wanted was to save us from destroying ourselves, you see, and in order to do that, first they had to understand our anatomy, and that's why they had chosen me, don't you see, they had singled me out to teach them about our species," she insisted, touching her throat, "and to give me the secret of our salvation, me of all people, you see, *me.*"

My sister had the good sense to keep mum about our baby-sitter's stories, but I was so razzled by hopes of meeting with these aliens and learning their world-saving secrets that I blabbed about the possibility to my mother, who quickly wormed the entire chronicle from me. We never visited Mrs. K. again, but often we would see her vacuuming the lawn in front of her house. "Utterly crazy," my mother declared.

Mrs. K. was not alone in her lunacy. Every year or so one of the career soldiers, having stared too long into the muzzle of his own gun, would go berserk or break down weeping. A guard began shooting deer from his jeep and leaving the carcasses in heaps on the roads. A janitor poured muriatic acid into the swimming pool and then down his own throat. One Christmastime, the lieutenant colonel who played Santa Claus started raving at the annual gift-giving and terrified the expectant children out of their wits. It took five fathers to muscle him down and make him quit heaving presents from his bag of gewgaws. To this day I cannot see Santa's white beard and red suit without flinching. Life on military reservations had also crazed many of the army wives, who turned to drink and drugs. Now and again an ambulance would purr into the Circle and cart one of them away for therapy. When at home, they usually kept hidden, stewing in bedrooms, their children grown and gone or off to school or buried in toys. Outside, with faces cracked like the leather of old purses, loaded up with consoling chemicals, the crazed women teetered carefully down the sidewalk, as if down a tightrope over an abyss.

The Arsenal fed on war and the rumors of war. When the Pentagon's budget was fat, the Arsenal's economy prospered. We could tell how good or bad the times were by reading our fathers' faces, or by counting the pickup trucks in the parking lots. The folks who lived just outside the chain-link fence in trailers and tarpaper shacks did poorly in the slow spells, but did just fine whenever an outbreak of Red Scare swept through Congress. In the lulls between wars, the men used to scan the headlines looking for omens of strife in the way farmers would scan the horizon for promises of rain.

In 1957, when the Arsenal was in the doldrums and parents were bickering across the dinner table, one October afternoon between innings of a softball game somebody read aloud the news about the launching of Sputnik. The mothers clucked their tongues and the fathers groaned; but soon the wise heads among them gloated, for they knew this Russian feat would set the loadlines humming, and it did.

Our model rocketeering took on a new cast. It occurred to us that any launcher capable of parking a satellite in orbit could plant an H-bomb in the Circle. If one of those bitter pills ever landed, we realized from our reading, there would be no Circle, no dallying deer, no forests, no Arsenal. Suddenly there were explosives above our heads as well as beneath our feet. The cracks in the faces of the crazed ladies deepened. Guards no longer joked with us as we passed through the gates to school. We children forgot how to sleep. For hours after darkness we squirmed on our beds, staring skyward. "Why don't you eat?" our mothers scolded. Aged thirteen or fourteen, I stood one day gripping the edge of the marble-topped table in our living room, staring through a glass bell at the spinning golden balls of an anniversary clock, and cried, "I don't ever want to be a soldier, not ever, ever!"

Each weekend in summer the soldiers still played war. They liked to scare up herds of deer with their tanks and pin them against a corner of the fence. Snooping along afterward, we discovered tufts of hair and clots of flesh caught in the barbed wire from the bucks that had leapt over. Once, after a weekend soldier's cigarette had set off a brushfire, we found the charred bodies of a dozen deer jammed against a fence. We filled ourselves with that sight, and knew what it meant. There we lay, every child in the Arsenal, every adult, every soul within reach of the bombs—twisted black lumps trapped against a fence of steel. I have dreamed of those charred deer ever since. During the war in Vietnam, every time I read or heard about napalm, my head filled with visions of those blackened lumps.

To a child, it seemed the only salvation was in running away. Parents and the family roof were no protection from this terror. My notebooks filled with designs for orbiting worlds that we could build from scratch and for rocket ships that would carry us to fresh, unpoisoned planets. But I soon realized that no more than a handful of us could escape to the stars; and there was too much on earth—the blue fountains of lilacs, the red streak of a fox across snow, the faces of friends—that I could never abandon. I took longer and longer walks through the backwoods of the Arsenal, soaking in the green juices; but as I grew older, the forest seemed to shrink, the fences drew in, the munitions bunkers and the desolate chemical dumps seemed to spread like a rash, until I could not walk far in any direction without stumbling into a reminder of our preparations for doom.

Because the foundations of old farms were vanishing beneath the tangle of barriers and saplings, for most of my childhood I had allowed myself to believe that nature would undo whatever mess we made. But the scars from these new chemicals resisted the return of life. The discolored dirt remained bare for years and years. Tank trucks spraying herbicides to save the cost of mowing stripped the roads and meadows of wildflowers. Fish floated belly-up in the scum of ponds. The shells of bird eggs, laced with molecules of our invention, were too flimsy to hold new chicks. The threads of the world were beginning to unravel.

In a single winter a hired trapper cleared out the beavers, which had been snarling the waterways, and the foxes, which had troubled the family dogs. Our own collie, brought as a puppy from Memphis, began to chase deer with a pack of dogs. At night he would slink back home with bloody snout and the smell of venison on his laboring breath. The guards warned us to keep him in, but he broke every rope. Once I saw the pack of them, wolves again, running deer across a field. Our collie was in the lead, gaining on a doe, and as I watched he bounded up and seized her by the ear and dragged her down, and the other dogs clamped on at the belly and throat. I preferred this wild killing to the shooting-gallery slaughter of the hunting season. If our own dogs could revert to wildness, perhaps there was still hope for the earth. But one day the guards shot the whole wolfish pack. Nature, in the largest sense of natural laws, would outlast us; but no particular scrap of it, no dog or pond or two-legged beast was guaranteed to survive.

There was comfort in the tales forever circulating among the children of marvelous deer glimpsed at dusk or dawn, bucks with white legs, a doe with pale fur in the shape of a saddle on her back, and, one year, a pair of ghostly albinos. Several of the children had seen the all-white deer. In 1962 I spent most of the

17

summer sunsets looking for them, needing to find them, hungering for these tokens of nature's prodigal energies. By September I had still seen neither hide nor hair of them. That October was the showdown over the placement of Soviet missiles in Cuba; Kennedy and Khrushchev squared off at the opposite ends of a nuclear street, hands hovering near the butts of their guns. For two weeks, while these desperadoes brooded over whether to start the final shooting, I quit going to school and passed all the hours of daylight outdoors, looking for those albino deer. Once, on the edge of a thicket, on the edge of darkness, I thought I glimpsed them, milky spirits, wisps of fog. But I could not be sure. Eventually the leaders of the superpowers lifted their hands a few inches away from their guns; the missiles did not fly. I returned to my studies, but gazed stupidly at every page through a meshwork of fear. In December the existence of the albino deer was proven beyond a doubt, for one afternoon in hunting season an Army doctor and his wife drove into the Circle with the pair of ghostly bodies tied onto the hood of their car.

The following year—the year when John Kennedy was killed and I registered for the draft and the tide of U.S. soldiers began to lap against the shores of Asia—my family moved from the Arsenal. "You'll sleep better now," my mother assured me. "You'll fatten up in no time." During the twelve years of our stay inside the chain-link fences, almost every night at suppertime outdated bombs would be detonated at the ammo dump. The concussion rattled the milkglass and willowware in the corner cupboard, rattled the forks against our plates, the cups against our teeth. It was like the muttering of local gods, a reminder of who ruled our neighborhood. From the moment I understood what those explosions meant, what small sparks they were of the engulfing fire, I lost my appetite. But even outside the Arsenal, a mile or an ocean away, every night at suppertime my fork still stuttered against the plate, my teeth still chattered from the remembered explosions. They still do. Everywhere now there are bunkers beneath the humped green hills; electronic challenges and threats needle through the air we breathe; the last wild beasts fling themselves against our steel boundaries. The fences of the Arsenal have stretched outward until they circle the entire planet. I feel, now, I can never move outside.

# COMING FROM THE COUNTRY

hen my family packed up and moved from the backwoods of Tennessee to the backwoods of Ohio I was not quite six years old. Like most children at that age I was still a two-legged smudge. Hardly a thing about me was definite except my way of talking, and that soon landed me in trouble. The kids in Ohio took one listen to my Tennessee accent and decided I was a hick. They let me know their opinion by calling me not only hick but hillbilly, ridge runner, clodhopper, and hayseed. (Our language provides about as many ways of calling somebody a yokel as of calling him a drunkard.) To my southern ears, *they* were the ones who sounded funny. But they had me outnumbered. So with cheerful cruelty they danced in circles around me and mimicked my drawl. In school, whenever I had to answer a teacher's question, they would echo my words and hoot with laughter. The only southerners they had met before were Kentuckians and West Virginians who had moved north when the Appalachian coal mines shut down. These Ohio kids lumped all southerners together under the heading of hillbillies, and regarded us all as the scum of the earth.

I wasn't comfortable in the role of scum of the earth. At first I tried fighting, swinging at anyone of any size who mocked me. The mockers gleefully hit back, of course. After having better sense pounded into me, I made a discovery that chameleons and turncoats have known for ages: I would be safer if I blended in.

From that time on, whatever the Ohio kids mimicked in my speech, I simply erased. Out went "you all," "I reckon," "rode a fur piece," and "tote a poke of taters." I quit saying my southern "Yes, Ma'am" and "No, Ma'am" to the teacher, who had labeled me a smart aleck for pretending such politeness. Before long I was talking like a Midwesterner, bland and cautious, as if I were cupping a marble on my tongue. It is the dialect I still speak, although when I'm tired, or telling stories, or visiting with my southern kinfolk, or feeling amorous, I slip back into the accents of Tennessee.

When my playmates quit mocking my speech, I thought I must surely have graduated from being a hick. But I had only quit sounding like a southern variety in order to begin sounding like a northern one; I had left one backwoods for another. In the years since that move to Ohio I've met enough purebred city people to realize that, however many layers of travel and booklearning I wear on my outside, down inside I am pure country. Since I'm now reasonably grown up, and still inwardly a yokel, I no longer expect to mature into a cosmopolitan. For better or worse, I come from the country, and lately I've begun to reflect on what this means.

Being a hick is less of a handicap than I once thought. It amuses my urban friends, it means I can leave my windows rolled down when I drive by pig farms, it allows me to ignore about half of what passes for modernity, and it supplies an excuse for a good many of my crotchets. Consider my habits of sleep, for example. I like to get up roughly when the sun does, and if sloth or a faulty alarm keeps me abed much later than seven I stumble through the day feeling out of sorts. This habit of rising early also means I turn into a sack of sawdust around ten o'clock at night, when my town friends want to go dancing. Knowing I'm a hick, they rib me a little and then let me shuffle off to bed.

Or consider—on my long list of rural crotchets—my dread of

21

taxis. I will carry a suitcase and walk any distance to avoid hiring a cab. The first time I ever had the chance of hiring one was at the age of seventeen, when I went away to college in Providence. Fresh off the Greyhound bus after a ride of forty-eight hours, lugging a year's supply of goods in my grandfather's sea chest, I asked a ticket-seller where I would find the university. He pointed up a hill, but said it was too far to walk hauling such a big trunk, so I'd better get a cab. I glanced warily at the row of dented yellow cars, each with its bubble on top and its flanks inscribed with the prices of various distances, then hefted the sea chest and trudged on up the hill. I haven't outgrown this phobia. Recently, in Baltimore, I was going out to dinner with some friends. Since there were nine of us, somebody ordered three taxis. Shy and backward, I stood aside while four of my friends got in the first cab and the remaining four piled into the second; when the last car drew up beside me I spun around and fled.

Now as it happens I enjoy using my legs and saving a dollar— two good reasons for avoiding cabs. But my difficulties with taxis lie deeper. I like to know where I'm going, and like to choose my own path for getting there. I hate sitting behind a driver who treats a crowded avenue as his private racetrack, shouting threats and blaring the horn. It is a torture for me to hear the meter tick and watch the odometer spin its numbers. I can't stand having time and distance parceled out that way, so many cents per click.

What bothers me even more, and not just in taxis, is to hire strangers to serve my needs. I don't like turning myself over to bellhops, waitresses, museum guides, barbers, or doctors unless I am on familiar territory and know the people I am dealing with. When I can't avoid staying in hotels, I mark myself out as a yokel by opening my own doors and carrying my own bags. I read the room service brochures with dismay. Imagine, leaving your dirty socks in the hallway and having them come back, discreetly per-fumed, in a plastic sack the next morning. Imagine, ringing for a glass of milk at midnight. It's as if, through room service, you're invited to become a child again, to be waited on hand and foot without the trouble of coming down with fever.

When I can't avoid going to a restaurant, I sit there with my plate full of food cooked by somebody I've never seen, I watch the frazzled waitress dashing between tables with a coffee pot, her bangs stringy from sweat, and I feel like getting up and giving her my chair. For me there is something shameful in being pampered and catered to by hirelings, a hint almost of slavery. And there is something craven in paying others to do what you could perfectly well do yourself.

Now you will not get very far or rise very high in a city if you refuse to have people wait on you. Foolish as it may be, this inhibition has stuck with me from my country upbringing. Lack of money and distance from town meant that we looked after ourselves; we shopped once a week, and otherwise made do with what was in the house; we fixed what broke. My father and mother between them could mend anything from bluejeans to banjos, from televisions to fishing tackle. We never used the yellow pages. If some job needed doing that we lacked the skills or the tools for—shoeing our ponies, cleaning a septic tank—we got a neighbor to do it, sometimes for money, sometimes for labor or a bushel of sweet corn or a jar of strawberry jam. There was no bragging attitude of self-sufficiency behind this. It was simply how we lived, and how I learned to live. In the country most children are taught to see to their own needs, and when they can't handle the job alone they hunt up a friend.

If you're used to fixing and patching and making-do, you need spare parts, which is why a lot of country places look like salvage yards, with discouraged cars up on blocks, disemboweled washing machines and cement mixers on the porch, coils of wire and stacks of wood under tarps by the barn. Stores are a long way off, they may not have the part you need, and anyway they'll charge you for it. Better keep every scrap of metal and plastic and wood you can lay your hands on. And if you started to build a house but ran out of money and strength after finishing the basement and you're living down there under ground, or if you're cramped inside a sixteen-foot trailer and hope one day to surround it with weathertight rooms, that's all the more reason for saving junk. To a pair of city eyes, such a place looks squalid. To the folks living at the center of that pile, it's neither ugly nor lovely; it's just there, an orchard of human fruits ready for plucking in season. Since I don't have much land around me these days, I've turned my basement into a junkyard. Down there you will find pieces from every machine that has ever failed me, sheets of plywood and plasterboard, tiles, bricks, blocks, switches, parts I can't name from gizmos I've forgotten.

The more I scavenge, the less I have to buy, which saves me confusion as well as money. When it comes to buying goods and services—the correct wine at dinner, a rental car, a shoeshine—city people always seem to me like clairvoyants, knowing every in and out, and I feel like an ignoramus. Take mixed drinks, for example. Everything I know about cocktails has to do with roosters. I come from a long line of drinkers, but whatever they drank came straight out of the bottle—beer, wine, whiskey. The first time I was roped into attending a fancy reception, I arrived hot and thirsty from a hard walk (avoiding taxis again), and a waiter sidled up to me with a trayful of drinks. It was plain he meant for me to take *something*, so I grabbed a glass of clear liquid and, thinking it was water, took an eager swig. It wasn't water. As nearly as I could figure, it was some concoction built around vodka. I held it in, but dared not speak for a long while.

The list of things I don't know how to buy is nearly as long as the list of things for sale. Digital stereos, lingerie for my wife, insurance, carpet, cheese. I find the ordering of meals especially grueling. My city friends know this instinctively, and so whenever I pay them a visit the first thing they say is, "Where shall we eat?" I suggest the kitchen, but they ignore me and begin reciting the names of ethnic restaurants. Even plain old American cafes

24

are a trial and tribulation to me. If there are more than seven items on the menu I'll have to choose by pointing with my eyes shut. And even with seven dishes, chances are that five will be utter mysteries to me. I would rather plant and grow the food than figure out how to order it.

I'm also hopeless at buying clothes. My twelve-year-old daughter says I dress like somebody out of a time-capsule. It is true my wardrobe hasn't changed much except in the size of collars and pants-legs since I turned eight. (I have heard rumors that men these days sometimes go without collars altogether, but I started with collars and am sticking by them.) The only time I'm *à la mode* is when I eat ice cream on pie. In my defensive moods— which come over me occasionally, like the flu—I repeat Thoreau's dictum: "beware of all enterprises that require new clothes, and not rather a new wearer of clothes." Like many folks whose tastes were formed in the boondocks, I'm not so much hostile to fashion as oblivious to it. The breezes of fashion blow hardest where people have time and money on their hands—two items in short supply in the country.

What I learned from growing up in the country is not how to buy things but how to *do* things: carpentry, plumbing, grafting, gardening, pruning, sewing, making hay with or without sunshine, cooking, canning, felling and planting trees, feeding animals and fixing machines, electrical wiring, plastering, roofing. There is a rude balance in effect here, which prevents me from understanding half of what my city friends are talking about when I stay with them, but enables me to fix their toaster and jumpstart their car. My clothes may be stodgy, but I can mend them. Restaurants may baffle me, but I know something about the raising of the cows and cabbages that appear under such mystifying aliases on the menu.

If I don't know how to do a job that needs doing in our household, my first thought is always to hunt up somebody who can teach me. To this day I still feel responsible for overhauling my house and car and for repairing whatever comes inside my four walls. This policy soon leads to grief. The second law of thermodynamics declares that entropy is on the increase everywhere, and the whole universe is drifting toward disorder. I can't vouch for the universe, but I know for sure that old houses and cheap cars fall apart faster than any mortal can patch them up. There are a great many more gadgets in my adult house than there were in my childhood one, and they break down in bafflingly novel ways. On the rear panels of most appliances, as you will have noticed, a label warns you not to remove the cover because there are no user serviceable parts inside. Instead, you are to ship the item off to qualified personnel, whose address, if provided at all, is usually in a city five hundred miles away. It galls me about as much to play the ignorant user as to play the scum of the earth. So when a gadget breaks down I brazenly undo the cover and poke about in the forbidden parts; and, lo and behold, about two-thirds of the time I can fix it. The other one-third of the time I am driven to despair.

My city friends avoid despair by renting apartments and turning their cars over to mechanics. Those brash enough to live in houses keep lists of plumbers, exterminators, chimney sweeps, handymen, painters, electricians, gardeners, a whole army of attendants. When anything needs tending, they reach for the phone. I keep no such list. Occasionally, in a panic, I will open the yellow pages, but I quickly shut them again without dialing, appalled by the mere thought of all those strangers waiting out there to serve me. Actually, I don't like using a phone at all. Not because I have any grudge against the instrument itself—I can fix a telephone—but because I like to see the folks I'm talking to. Without a face and a breath attached to speech, I grow uneasy. It's like eating when you have a cold and can taste nothing.

Pushed to its ugly extreme, this cleaving of the world between neighbors and strangers becomes tribalism, a disease that is common in the country. I have seen crosses burning on the lawns of

26

integrated schools, have listened to slander against Jews and Italians and Hispanics, have watched factory workers beat imported strike-breakers with shovels. I have been an outsider in too many places myself to underestimate the dangers of tribalism. But the prejudices of country people are limited by ignorance; you can't very well hate nations or religions you've never heard tell of. The crazy-quilt mixture of peoples in a metropolis may lead to wise tolerance, or it may lead to a more comprehensive brand of bigotry. I once knew a Chicago doctor, a descendant of the Old Testament Assyrians, whose roster of enemies included such Biblical remnants as Chaldeans, Babylonians, and Mesopotamians, as well as Zoroastrians and Swedenborgians.

This business of neighbors and strangers touches on another of my country oddities. My city friends describe their glee in watching eccentrics perform on street corners, in subways, in the lobbies of skyscrapers. The shaggy old man who wears a sandwich board and drools in his beard and proclaims the end of the world is a source of entertainment for them, part of the urban spectacle. But the sight of him makes me ache. I feel my way inside his dingy hide and share his apocalyptic dread. Mind you, I don't sidle up and talk with him. I keep my distance, afraid he might lay on me some enormous claim. By the end of a day in the city, identifying with drunks and prophets and twitching zombies, unable to help a single one of them, I feel battered and drained.

Back in my country childhood, there were so few people around that every one of them stood out for me as a person. The local eccentrics were also neighbors; I went to school with their children, picked apples for them, stood beside them in the hardware store, listened to their harangues on our front porch. I knew their life histories and learned, often, what ill wind had turned their minds in strange directions. To meet derelicts I didn't have to go cruising through the Bowery, or dress up in rags like George Orwell and sneak into a Parisian flophouse; there were

27

derelicts enough living on our road, squirreled away in trailers and tarpaper shacks.

Our local prophet of doom was a carpenter with five children, one of whom, a gawky boy, was in my class at school. Every crazy word from the father left a shadow on the face of the son. When the carpenter received his message that the world was about to end, he stopped work on the family house, which was half-built, quit all his other jobs, and withdrew his children from school. As the date announced for the earth's demise drew near, the prophet grew frenzied, surrounded as he was by skeptics and sinners, and eventually he landed in jail. After the date passed and the world survived, the father was set free, but he never finished his house, never unbent from God's stiff wind; and the face of his son, my classmate, never uncrimped from the pain.

My trouble is, I hate turning other people into a spectacle, as if human beings were two-dimensional figures in a mural. For a short while I exult in the city's million faces; but soon those faces become as indistinguishable to me as dewdrops on the morning grass, and then I hurry back to a place where people are rare enough to have features and names. This withdrawal troubles my city friends. How can I survive without getting a daily look at Afghans or Sikhs? They count upon seeing the costumes and complexions of two dozen nationalities on their ride to work each morning. I will grant there is pleasure and the chance of wisdom in observing that human display. I say a chance rather than a certainty, because I notice that most of my friends do no more than look at these colorful strangers, never so much as exchange a word with them, and rarely see the same mysterious face two days running. I'm not convinced there is more pleasure or wisdom to be had from glimpsing two dozen nationalities of *homo sapiens* than from encountering on a day's walk fifty species of plants and animals. Do we have to stretch ourselves farther to appreciate a Tibetan, say, than to appreciate a turtle or a trillium? Notice I'm not saying that a wildflower is deeper or nobler than a

Buddhist monk, but that a flower's inwardness is further from our
own. When all is said and done, despite its heady mix of peoples,
the city is filled with versions of ourselves; the country is likelier
to confront us with true otherness.

I think we all could stand a good dose of otherness, to tell you
the truth. I think we are far too full of ourselves. Walk around in a
city, and everything you see, even the sickly tree corseted in an
iron grate or the dog on a leash, is there by human design or
sufferance. What wizards we are! Look at those skyscrapers! Listen to the roar of those engines in our concrete canyons! Behold
the wonders for sale behind the plateglass windows! The execu-
tives who make the decisions that shape our lives gaze down from
gleaming towers onto that scene. How can they help but regard
themselves as gods?

You may point to museums and open-air markets—places I
love to visit—but I believe the city's pure essence shows in office
towers and shopping malls. Deep in the architects who design
these enclosures and in the enthusiasts who frequent them—the
skyscraper addicts and mall zealots—there is a horror of the nonhuman. A shopping mall is a space-age Garden of Eden. Everything needful sprouts on the shelves of stores, as if by spon-
taneous generation, lights defy the cycles of day and night,
windows keep out bugs, and overhead the arched roof shuts out
weather and wildness. Push the shopping mall one degree further and you have Disneyland, the urban dream of nature: ster-
ilized dirt, paved walkways, rivers that flow in circles and never
flood, mechanical beasts that roar on signal, grass and flowers
chastened into purity by chemicals.

It is easy to pretend, in a city, that humans have made the
world and dwell there alone. In the country, you know better. It's
the difference between living in *a* creation and living in *the* creation. Life in the boondocks discourages you from claiming with a
straight face that humans are omnipotent. If you think our works
are mighty and permanent, drive down any back road and study

the caved-in barns, the cellar holes grown up in thickets. If you begin to doubt we have companions on spaceship earth, try clearing a patch of ground beside a woods and gardening for a summer. Insects and worms and rabbits and raccoons and possums and beasts you never identify will gobble your plants; weeds and forest seedlings will sprout between your neat rows. Go away for a month and when you come back the woods will be occupying your garden plot. Of course we have devised ways of discouraging rabbits and chickweed. The manufacturers of poisons sell brews that snuff out everything except what we suffer to live—brews that incidentally, and more slowly, snuff us out as well. But this very willingness to poison whatever obstructs our schemes is a symptom of the arrogance for which life in the country is a good antidote.

When Hamlet speaks to Ophelia of "country matters," he means sex, fertility, the old sashay of the flesh. What else could the Prince of Denmark know about the backwoods? City people often think of the land rolling beyond the last streetlight as one vast breeding ground for soybeans and mistletoe, pulpwood and hogs. The folks who make their lives out there seem, from the city, more like pigs and pines than humans. When a writer needs a character to symbolize the animal within us—think of D. H. Lawrence, Tennessee Williams—he's likely to drag in a bumpkin with muddy boots and rural twang. If you write a novel about the backwaters and hope to make a splash in the metropolis, you had better feature incest and idiots.

Of course things do breed in the country—otherwise neither Hamlet nor the rest of us would have a bite to eat. And of course rural kids don't have to wait for high school health class or a chat with Mom and Dad to learn the alphabet of sex. I learned the rudiments with a bang, long before I was in a position to apply the knowledge, by raising rabbits. I observed the mechanics on a large scale every time we took one of our mares to visit the stud. I tassled corn and helped pollinate squash by poking the flowers with a feather. This knowledge of how animals and plants go about their business has not kept me from greatly enjoying the human version. If anything, it has deepened my pleasure to know that my loving a woman, and the whole amazing edifice of romance, is raised on such sturdy foundations.

It's true that culture is stretched pretty thin in the sticks. If you can't get through the week without seeing an opera or visiting an art gallery, you had better stay in the metropolis. I've noticed that my city friends are mostly consumers of culture, not creators, buying their way in just as they buy their groceries. Sometimes they talk as though a season ticket to the ballet makes them bearers of Western Civilization. Because the human net is spread so thin in the countryside, you realize you must help make and sustain it. Whatever happens on the back roads and in small towns—carnivals and spelling bees, parades and horse races, bluegrass concerts, open air theatricals—happens because people you know, or you yourself, make it happen. It is do-it-yourself culture, homely to be sure, but heartfelt and sprung from local talent.

In the country, if things go undone, you can't blame officials. I know a carpenter who didn't see the point of joining the volunteer fire department until one day his barn started to smoke. His wife called the emergency number, a siren went off, and pretty soon the neighbors turned up with their pumper and hoses. They held off spraying long enough for the chief to ask, "What do you think about volunteering now?" and for the carpenter to reply, "I think now's a real good time." So he joined on the spot, grabbed a hose, and has remained a loyal volunteer ever since. It's good to feel responsible for the place you inhabit, and easier to feel that responsibility when the place is thinly settled.

Marx and Engels, those two quintessential urban visionaries, promised in their Communist manifesto that the world revolution would free all hicks and yokels from "rural idiocy." As someone who inherited a good dose of rural idiocy, I have to admit there is a core of truth in this contemptuous phrase. When I work all day in the sun pitching hay or driving nails or splitting wood, I slump down at night and live wholly in my body. On those nights the neighborhood dogs have livelier thoughts than I do. With or without a revolution, I'll remain backward and countrified. I'll never be urbane—the very word a reminder of how we equate refinement with the city. I'll never feel at ease living where the glare of lights keeps me from seeing the stars and where fear of strangers keeps me from walking out at night. A Tennessee ridgerunner accent still underlies my Midwestern prairie tones, a dirt-road soul shows through cracks in the paving of my education. The pleasures and knowledge that come to those of us who grew up in the country may be small potatoes compared to what city breeding offers, but in the long cold winter of cruelty and want that lies ahead for the world, we'll need all the potatoes we can find.

# LISTENING TO OWLS

**O**n the morning after the winter solstice, two hours before sunrise, moon full, I stood on frozen feet beside a pine grove in southern Indiana and listened for owls. The pine boughs were dark featherings on darkness. Every winter weed and bush in the meadow cast a pale moon-shadow. Burst milkweed pods hung upon last year's stems like giant commas. Breath haloed about my face in the five-degree air. In such stillness an owl could hear the footpads of mice, the rustling of rabbits, but I with my clumsy ears could hear nothing.

The friend who had brought me to this owl country—Don Whitehead, a husky man with sun-creases around his eyes, who indulges his passion for the outdoors by teaching ecology—cupped gloved hands to his mouth and uttered a long cry, rather like the noise a strangled rooster might make. This was the barred owl's call, which bird books will tell you sounds like a guttural rendering of "Who cooks for you, who cooks for you all?" But don't let the cozy sentences fool you. The cry of the barred owl, even the counterfeit cry my friend Don was making, resembles no human speech. It is night-speech. So there we stood, on the longest night of the year, two grown men hooting into the darkness and listening.

Presently a cow answered, lowing mournfully. Next a dog yapped, then two more, then a fourth, all at a great distance from us and seemingly from all four points of the compass. We were surrounded by domestication. When a rooster chimed in, I began to despair of owls. Gingerly, afraid my iced toes might shatter, I rocked from foot to foot.

Don motioned for me to keep still. Dogs, cow, and rooster obligingly hushed. A moonlit smile stole across his face. He pointed, away from the pine woods and across the meadow, toward a cedar-topped ridge. I faced where he pointed, shut my eyes, and listened, listened so hard my shivering body grew calm. What I heard sounded at first like a distant creek splashing over rocks. I disappeared into my listening. The water-sound grew sharper, divided into syllables, spoke to me at last in the sixty-million-year-old voice of an owl.

Sixty million years is only an estimate, of course, and might be off by an eon or two. The bones of owls, like those of all other birds, are hollow and flimsy, and consequently make poor fossils. Reading the rocks, scientists find dinosaurs by the truckload, seashells and gigantic ferns by the long ton, but scant trace of birds. Some dinosaurs had wings, but they must have been clumsy fliers. Maybe they could not truly fly, but had to climb trees or cliffs and then leap in one hungry swoop onto their prey.

Some one hundred and eighty million years ago, one of these winged dinosaurs lay down in the mud and left its fossilized imprint, including a toothed jaw, a long bony tail, and the ghostly trace of feathers. Feathers! Here was a new invention, and a durable one, to judge by the chickadee on my windowsill. Life shoving through the sluggish bodies of dinosaurs—so the scientists theorize—chopped off the heavy tail, feathered the wings, hollowed the bones, and eventually produced birds. Holding dinosaur and bird together in the mind takes some getting used to: a lumbering swamp monster on one side and an ounce of fluff on the other, with a dotted line connecting them. But next time you get close to a pigeon or some other patient bird, next time you clean a chicken, notice the reptilian scales on its legs and see if you don't catch a whiff of ancient mud.

While the barred owl called, I shook, as if I were a plucked string. Of course the five-degree weather probably had something to do with my shaking. But mainly it was that night-voice plucking at the strings of wonder and dread in me. Listening in that moon shadowed meadow, the grasses and weeds curling from the soil like delicate brush strokes, I understood why so many ancient peoples regarded the owl's cry as an omen of death.

In the old days, when the Chinese heard that cry, they called it "digging a grave" and knew an owl was on its way to snatch some dying soul. Australian aborigines believed that owls trafficked only in the souls of women, the souls of men being reserved for bats. Sicilians used to say that an owl cry meant an ailing person would die within three days. If nobody in the neighborhood was sick, then somebody would come down with tonsil trouble. No point in wasting an evil omen. The Old Testament warned the Israelites not to eat owls, lumping them with vultures as pariahs of the wastelands. Sumerians and Hebrews associated owls with Lilith, the goddess of death, who struck in the night. In the Middle Ages this death-dealing hag became a witch, and the owl one of her familiars, a worker of wickedness.

"Death's dreadful messenger"—that's what Edmund Spenser called the bird. And Shakespeare found it difficult to murder anyone on stage without the help of a preliminary announcement from owls. The king's murder in *Macbeth*, for example, is accompanied by the shriek of an owl, "the fatal bellman which gives the stern'st goodnight."

Even the word *owl* is funereal, coming as it does from a Latin root meaning "to howl," the same root that gives us *ululation* (the sound of wailing and lamentation). The birds have not helped their reputation any by showing a fondness for nesting in ruins and graveyards. Their flight is silent, thanks to the downy edge of their primary feathers and oversized wings. Like death, they arrive unannounced and gobble their victims whole.

These are not comforting details to recollect at two hours before sunrise, with your extremities frozen and ice forming in your arteries and the whole universe seized by a winter that might last forever—not comforting at all, especially if you are given, as I am, to brooding about death even in daylight and without the aid of owls.

Don yelped his strangled-rooster cry again. I flinched. He grinned. Not at me, it turned out, but at the voice of a second barred owl that joined the first in a courting duet. The twin songs spiraled about one another, twisting the birds together in a rope of desire. At the far end of that rope, if things worked out, would be a nest, eggs, four weeks of incubation, and two or three owlets looking like handfuls of dandelion fluff. So here were voices crying at the other gate, the gate of birth rather than death. Night and eros also go together. A century ago, in the streets of London, if you had inquired about "owls" you would have been led to a brothel. Night hags bring the big death; nightwalkers bring the small one.

Once they tuned up, our pair of lovers kept hooting yearnfully, like Romeo and Juliet in their balcony scene. What business did I have eavesdropping on this erotic serenade? How would I like finding them perched one midnight on my bedroom windowsill, their radar-dish ears catching every rustle of my sheets? But I had no intention of budging from that icy meadow so long as they kept singing. Now that love had been introduced, I could hear enough gaiety in their call to understand why Audubon, trailing barred owls in the swamps of Louisiana, compared their cry "to the affected bursts of laughter which you may have heard from some of the fashionable members of our own species."

If you listen to recordings of owls you will hear an eerie babel of moans and cackling, snores and screeches. There are about one hundred thirty species worldwide in sizes ranging from sparrow to eagle, and they speak in as many dialects as people do. Some of the voices are liquid trills. Others resemble the harsh buzz of locusts. Some make you think of murder victims, sirens, the sickening squeal cars make before a crash. Defending their nests, many owls snap their bills, clicking like Geiger counters. Burrowing owls, which like to set up house in abandoned prairie dog tunnels, scare away predators by hissing like a rattlesnake. With wings spread and tail ruffled, a hissing owl might remind other predators rather uncomfortably of a wildcat. Saw-whet owls derive their name from the saw-sharpening whine they make. More than one early traveler in the American wilderness reports having been fooled by this bird whistle into thinking a sawmill was just ahead.

Owls do all this muttering for purposes of courtship, as our yearnful pair of barreds were doing, and also for establishing territory. Wolves mark out the boundaries of their turf by urinating and defecating. Humans build fences and guard-posts. Owls, more fastidious than either, embroider the edges of their territory with song. They also fly their boundaries, regular as mailmen. When threatened, they will cry out like sirens to announce alarms. Nestlings clamor for food in the universally raucous manner of the young. Nocturnal owls often sing for a spell at dusk before the evening's hunt, like children at hide-and-seek counting to twenty before going in search of victims.

They probably conduct other business with their hoots and gurgles—commenting on the weather, say, or estimating the population of field mice. Altogether, the vocabulary of owls is about as complex as that of the average telephone conversation.

Once you've spoken about hunger and fear, weather and territory, sex and death, what more is there to say?

Listening to screech owls beside Walden Pond, Thoreau was reminded of wailing women and mournful lovers, as if their call
"were the dark and tearful side of music." Others have heard
melancholy in these voices. The Kootenay Indians used to warn
that children crying in the night would be mistaken by owls for
their own young and be carried away. (I tried this warning on my
three-year-old, but he seemed to like the idea of being snatched
out of bed and flown high above the night-country.) A brooding
and sometimes melancholy bird himself, Thoreau welcomed the
screech owls, saying, "They give me a sense of the variety and
capacity of that nature which is our common dwelling."

Screech owls do not actually screech, but gently whinny, or
give a voiceless, quavering whistle like the syncopated whoosh-
ing sound of a revolving door. Fans of science-fiction movies
might be reminded of the sounds flying saucers are supposed to
make. My friend Don had perfected that call as well. He had
spent his teen years in the Adirondacks imitating birds, the way
ordinary teenagers imitate television comedians or rock singers.
When the barred owls tired of their love-duet and fell silent, Don
gave a tremulous whistle. Within moments a screech owl whis-
tled back, as if to say, "I thought you'd never call." This time the
voice rose from the pine woods, so we shifted around to face the
shaggy boughs. It would most likely be a solitary male, staking
out his territory. The whistling came only once more. Here I am,
he was announcing. This is my realm of bugs and frogs and field
mice. Don spoke back to him, but the owl apparently had said his
say. The pines bristled silently in the moonlight.

Audubon once carried a live screech owl in his coat pocket
from Philadelphia to New York, over land and water, feeding it by
hand. Audubon did things like that. On one occasion he was pre-
sented with a live duck. Lacking any other place to store it, he

carried the bird half a day under his top hat. (I specify that both duck and owl were alive, since Audubon's ordinary method of studying birds, like that of all early ornithologists, was to shoot first and ask scientific questions later. "I have not shot but have seen a Hawk of great size entirely *new*" he wrote to his wife from Florida, and then added hopefully, "may perhaps kill him tomorrow." He sometimes shot upwards of three hundred birds to secure one fine specimen for illustration.) He once fell into quicksand while chasing a great horned owl. The slime was up to his armpits before someone heard his cries and pulled him out. Audubon held no grudge against the bird, to judge from his portrait of a male and female pair. They stare at you regally from the page, "ear" tufts erect, yellow-rimmed eyes somewhat crossed, feathers subtle as fine-threaded tapestry.

Studying those eyes, you can see where owls get their reputation for wisdom. We guess at the intelligence of strangers by watching their eyes. Here are two strangers, these Audubon owls, who bore holes through you with their stare. You could use either face for a mantra and lose yourself among the concentric rings of feathers. Their eyes proclaim that they know exactly who they are and what they are about. They have seen to the heart of things, while we grope around on the surface. Since the eyes of owls are fixed in their sockets, the bird must swivel its entire head in order to look to the side or rear. You receive no sly glances from an owl, but always a full stare. Its neck is so flexible that it can even gaze directly behind itself, thus keeping watch on the past. When a cartoon owl gazes at me and poses its cartoon question—"Whooo?"—I wish I had as clear an answer as the owl appears to have. Like all wild creatures, owls are serenely and unambiguously themselves. They do not suffer from existential angst. They do not wake themselves up four hours early and fly into town in hopes of hearing the overtones of truth in human chatter.

But are owls wise? The Greeks thought so, identifying them

with Athena, goddess of wisdom. In medieval illustrations, owls accompany Merlin and share in his sorcery. In fairy tales they rival the fox for cunning. Children's picture books show them wearing spectacles, mortarboard, and scholar's gown. Soups and other confections made from owls have been credited with curing whooping cough, drunkenness, epilepsy, famine, and insomnia. The Cherokee Indians used to bathe their children's eyes with a broth of owl feathers to keep the kids awake at night. Recipes using owl eggs are reputed to bestow keen eyesight and wisdom. Yet these birds are no smarter, ornithologists assure us, than most others—and other birds don't set a very high standard.

A museum guide in Boston once displayed a drowsy-looking barn owl on his gloved wrist, explaining to those of us assembled there how small the bird's brain actually was. "You'll notice the head of this live specimen appears to be about the size of a grapefruit," he said, "but it's mostly feathers." Lifting his other hand, which cradled a round ball of bone, he added, "the skull, you see, is the size of a lemon. There's only room enough inside for a bird-brain, not enough for Einstein!" We all laughed politely. But I was not convinced. Sure, the skull was small. The lower half was devoted to jaw and most of the upper half to beak and eyeholes. Yet enough neurons could be fitted into the remaining space to enable the barn owl to catch mice in total darkness. They can even snatch bats on the wing, these princes of nighttime stealth. We had to invent sonar for locating submarines, radar for locating airplanes; neither is much use with mice or bats. Barn owls can also see dead—and therefore silent—prey in light one-hundredth as bright as we would need. Like the ability to saw a board square or judge the consistency of bread dough, that might not amount to scholarship, but it is certainly a wisdom of the body. It has worked for some sixty million years. Farmers in Scandinavia, not caring about IQ, often build roosts and special doors near the peaks of their barns for these efficient rodent-killers.

I'm afraid we give owls credit for wisdom chiefly because they look like us. Behold the rounded head, the prominent eyes set in front, a disk of feathers radiating outward from each eye like cheeks, dark slashes across the forehead like eyebrows, the lethal beak protruding only far enough to resemble a nose. Aha, we think, here are feathered, midget versions of ourselves; they must be smart. I suppose the owls, noting the same resemblance, would assume we are expert killers, and they would be right.

You can't judge owls by appearance. Their daytime faces— glimpsed in zoos and museums and books, occasionally on birds I discover at their perches—don't match the nighttime voices Don and I were hearing. The face of a screech owl could belong to Cotton Mather or some other Puritan divine, full of wrath and fiery judgment; yet its whistle falls as forgivingly as rain. Round facial markings make the barred owl look like a pilot in goggles, jet-black eyes fresh from outer space, rotund head filled with unearthly lore. Yet when I hear the "Who cooks for you, who cooks for you all?" cry, I can only think of lovers yodeling beneath balconies or strangling from disappointment. Barn owls, with faces pale and heart-shaped as old valentines, look like sad elves. But their repertoire of cries includes a screech that will set your teeth on edge and stiffen your neck hairs.

One of these elfin-looking barn owls once scared me nearly witless. I was camping with some other boys on a ridge overlooking the Mahoning River in northern Ohio. The sun was down. We'd made a fire, the light splashing on the undersides of sycamore leaves, and while we sat with our backs toward the dark woods, my father was telling us a ghost story. I can't remember the gory details, but the story climaxed with a squadron of ghouls pouncing on some unsuspecting boys as they sat around a campfire. "And the blood-drinking ghosts hooked their claws in the sycamore bark," my father was whispering, "and they spied down on those poor boys, kind of sizing them up. And then the ghosts

41

tilted forward just a little bit on the sycamore limbs, and they—
JUMPED!" We jumped. Then *he* jumped, as a scream burst over
our heads, so loud it seemed to crack the night open. My heart
quit, lungs quit, brain played turtle in my skull. I was doing my
best to imitate a rock, so the blood-sucking ghouls would nab the
guy next to me. Only when the scream sounded again, farther
away, down along the river, did I open my eyes. The other boys
looked like prisoners of war, like pale stowaways who had just
come blinking onto deck. My father's voice still shook as he explained, "It was just a barn owl. I expect we scared it off its
roost."

Don and I heard no barn owls on the night of the winter solstice.
Never common in the Middle West, this prowler has become
even scarcer in recent years because of pesticide poisoning. Like
all predators, owls are near the top of the food chain, and so they
gobble toxins in concentrated doses. We're predators, too, feeding on the whole of nature. Although we don't eat owls, we poison them, with chemicals designed to protect our corn from
worms, our apples from blemishes. One price of the perfection
we expect on our dinner table is the death of night-hunters, the
death of singers, the death of birds that impersonate ghosts.

We did hope to rouse a great-horned owl before daylight. Don
knew a likely place, a hillside planted to sweetgum and pine,
about a mile from the ridge where we had listened to the barred
and screech owls. So we hiked the mile on ice-cake feet, scaring
up a rabbit and meadowlark along the way. Although the sun was
rising, the temperature wasn't. The messages coming from my
hands and feet were as shrill as the static on a shortwave radio
during electrical storms.

By the time we reached the hillside, both eastern and western
horizons were glowing, with rising sun and setting moon. The
tips of pines and cedars fretted the skyline like saw-teeth. It was a
dangerous hour, this lull between night and day, for any beast

small enough to become owl food. Rabbits, squirrels, porcupines, skunks, mice and rats, snakes and all manner of birds—any of these might provide breakfast for the great horned owl. Here is a formidable bird, growing to a height of two feet and a wingspan of nearly five, capable of killing (but not carrying) animals that outweigh it. Pound-for-pound—as announcers say about bantam-weight boxers—this character is fiercer than a mountain lion. Any sort of owl is likely to get mobbed in daytime if smaller birds find it roosting. But great horneds drive crows into a particular frenzy. I once saw fifteen of those braggart birds pestering a great horned owl, diving and jabbering at him until he suddenly lashed out with a taloned foot and set a ragged clump of feathers tumbling. Unenlightened, the fourteen survivors resumed their pestering, and the owl dispatched two more before they left. If you have the bad luck or bad judgment to climb into its nesting tree while the youngsters are about, the great horned will greet you with a wallop and give your head and arms a good raking.

A friend of mine, a gangling man who assembles color televisions for a living and who has lost two wives because of his passion for birding, told me about meeting a great horned owl in a tulip tree. He had climbed the tree before dawn to wait to photograph the sunrise over Lake Monroe. There he perched, on a morning warmer than the one Don and I had picked for owling, his legs straddling a limb and his back against the trunk. Presently, the branch just above his head shook, as if someone had given it a single karate chop. Looking up, he saw the solemn bird. It was scanning the territory, head tilted forward and slowly pivoting, ear-tufts raised like twin antennae, saucer eyes making a murderous survey of the lakeside. When it spied my friend, the owl glanced casually away, and then did a comical double-take. For a moment the two perchers stared eye-to-eye, the man calculating whether there was light enough for a photo, the bird probably calculating whether this gawky beast would do for breakfast. Evidently deciding no, the owl gave a noncommittal hoot and flew away. My friend was lucky this was a hunting rather than a nesting tree, for had he approached the nest, the bird would probably have mauled him.

The great horned owl typically gives a gurgling call of one, two, and then three notes, as if it were learning to count. Don, as you might have predicted, can gurgle convincingly, and did so on that brightening hillside. No answer. He tried again and again, pausing between calls, but the great horned owls had apparently clocked out for the night. I was so ecstatic with sunrise and moonset, so intoxicated with the night-voices we had already heard, that I would have turned entirely to ice before giving up on this last of our neighborhood owls. Don patiently crowed, I rocked on numb legs, the sun opened in the east like the mouth of a furnace. At last a gurgling voice answered from the woods. When I finally distinguished the sound, I realized I had been hearing it for several minutes, but had not recognized it amid the wind noises and the chatter of awakening songbirds. Guessing the direction, I peered intently, hoping to catch a glimpse of the bird. The song unraveled for five minutes or more, and then came to an abrupt end. In the first moment of quiet I saw a huge shadow rise above the treetops, wings large enough for an angel. It flapped once, twice, and then swerved and was gone. I blinked, wondering if I had really seen it, or had only conjured it out of the dawn sky. But Don had seen it, too. Beside me he was murmuring, "Wonderful, wonderful!"

When I try to explain to friends why I rise so early on a December day to go shiver in the owl-haunted woods, I find that those who have to ask my reasons cannot be made to understand them. When you sit near a waterfall, with the mist playing over your skin and the roar shaking your spine, you either realize that this is one of the authentic experiences, one of the touchstones for all living, or you don't. If you don't feel that thrill in the presence of a waterfall, or a stand of virgin timber, or a mountain peak, or a calling owl, then no explanation on earth will make you feel it.

Think of it, carrying on half of a love-duet with a bird. There you stand in your human shape, flightless and nightblind, conversing with a killer that navigates through darkness. Our literature and film are crowded with aliens from outer space, tentacled and bug-eyed, possessed of mysterious powers. But is any of these extraterrestrials stranger than an owl? Until visitors actually arrive from some remote planet, let me talk with owls or whales or even Sufis, and I will find my conversation alien enough. Such talk makes *us* the visitors, the invaders from ultima Thule. The owl cannot speak in our tongue, but we can speak in his. The creation lures us out of ourselves, while the owl remains tucked snugly in the pouch of his instincts. He only speaks to us because we have entered his precinct, gone out to meet him, put off for a while our human garments and assumed his.

Chilled and triumphant, Don and I hiked back toward the car, neither of us speaking, as if we had tacitly agreed to keep the owls in our ears as long as possible. Our path took us along the shore of the lake, where cattails and reeds stood rigid in a frozen border of ice. In the deeper parts, waves lapped against the hem of ice with the sound of polite applause. In the shallow bays, where ice glinted like gunmetal from shore to shore, steam rising from the surface turned rose and violet in the early sunlight. It was like the smoke from incense, an offering fit for owl-gods or any other deities. Here and there a whirlwind lifted columns of steam twenty or thirty feet into the air. The spouts trailed across the ice, sinuous as snakes, and then collapsed back into the lower mists.

As the light grew stronger, I noticed that near the lake's edge the black ice was covered with a rough white fur. Bending closer, I could see that the fur was really a miniature forest of ice crystals, each crystal fern-shaped, a tiny glistening lattice. The boughs of this frozen forest were so delicate that they swayed

45

when I breathed on them. The tallest thicket of crystals was no higher than the knuckle on a flattened hand, yet within those pygmy thickets was more intricacy than the eye could follow.

Every weed and twig on the shore was covered with the same fragile wafers of ice. I plucked a stem of foxtail grass and held it between me and the sun. The light shattered on the crystals as I gently twirled the stem; a sliver of ice, thinner than an eyelash, broke the glow from a hydrogen explosion into rainbows. Soon the frost on my foxtail melted. Before my very eyes the ice forest was evaporating from the margins of the lake, a disappearing trick more astonishing than any Saturday-afternoon magic. The mists and spouts over the frozen bays were thinning away. I wanted to seize this moment of ice-beauty, hold it still for my perpetual delight. But it would not linger, anymore than the owls would.

All the way up the hillside, whenever I turned to face the sun, I saw ice crystals needling through the air. Blown or shaken loose from trees, they drifted slantwise like silver seeds, like migrating sparks.

We heard, arising from somewhere near the car, the raucous scolding of blue jays. "They're pestering something," said Don.

"A hawk?" I guessed.

"Or an owl, maybe."

Putting off our weariness, we clumped on numb legs toward the noise. There were six or eight jays swooping and squawking about the hollow crown of a dead beech.

"That's got to be an owl tree," Don whispered.

At our approach, the jays spiraled away, screeching indignantly. Don and I circled the beech in opposite directions, eyes alert for any movement in the tree's rot-blackened top. But we met on the far side of the circle without having spied anything.

"You go beat on the trunk with a stick," Don suggested, "and I'll keep watch."

"How would a great horned owl, say, feel about somebody come knocking on his tree?" I asked.

"He wouldn't like it one bit," Don allowed.

"What's he likely to do about it?"

The creases about Don's eyes deepened. "He's likely to come out fast," he said, "too fast for messing with you or me, and then he's going to disappear in about half a blink."

Still wary, I picked up a thick branch from the ground, approached the hollow beech, and gave the trunk a polite thwack.

"Hit it hard," Don urged.

So I grasped the stick with both hands and slammed the tree a few home-run blows. Between strokes I glanced up, to catch a glimpse of anything that might fly from the rotten peak. Or anything that might come plummeting down on me, talons lowered for the kill. Nothing flew, nothing plummeted.

After a few more thumps, Don called, "It's no use. If the jays had an owl in there, it was gone before we got here."

I dropped the stick, feeling a little ashamed, as if, in the daylight, I had tried to summon up by brute force what only patience and stillness had been able to summon up in the darkness. The hollow beech was a reminder, if I needed a reminder, that owls will not be bullied. You can hoot at them until you're blue in the face, but they will only answer when they please, if they please. Talking with them is like soliciting a word from the gods. There are rituals to be observed, such as choosing the right season of year and time of day. Certain owl-callers, like certain priests, enjoy better luck than others. But after you have made all your preparations, you can only wait. If the owls choose to remain invisible and silent, then, like the gods, silent and invisible they will remain. There are no switches you can throw to make them perform. They fly their own missions, speak their own messages, with no more regard for us than the moon has.

From the car, I turned to look back down at the lake. The mists had now almost all dissolved away into daylight. The whirlwinds of steam had ceased their revels. In the ragged patches of open water near the middle of the lake, a few ducks and geese congregated. The two bald eagles spotted here this season would find the hunting poor. Another week of freezing weather would close the lake entirely, driving water birds south and the eagles after them. But the owls would stay on. Adaptable, stealthy, expert at killing and not overly particular about what they eat, they would endure. By keeping to the nightside, owls avoid their one dangerous enemy—us, lords of the dayside. So long as there are woods, and not too many poisons, there will be owls. So long as there are owls, we can hear night-voices and remain humble.

"I rejoice that there are owls," says Thoreau. "Let them do the idiotic and maniacal hooting for men. It is a sound admirably suited to swamps and woods which no day illustrates, suggesting a vast and undeveloped nature which men have not recognized." Most of us still don't recognize that "undeveloped nature," that nature which dances and unfurls its life without regard to human purposes. We can't hear the earth sing above all the racket our species makes. Listening to owls is a remedy for such deafness.

# CLOUD CROSSING

**C**louds are temporary creatures. So is the Milky Way, for that matter, if you take the long entropic view of things. I awake on a Saturday in mid-October with the ache of nightmares in my brain, as if I have strained a muscle in my head. Just a week before I turn thirty-three, just a month before my son turns one, I do not need physics or nightmares to remind me that we also are temporary creatures.

Baby Jesse is changing cloud-fast before my eyes. His perky voice begins pinning labels on dogs and bathtubs and sun. When I say, "Want to go for a walk?" on this morning that began with nightmares of entropy, he does not crawl towards me as he would have done only a few days ago. He tugs himself upright with the help of a chair, then staggers toward me like a refugee crossing the border, arms outstretched, crowing, "Wa! Wa!"

So I pack baby and water and graham crackers into the car, and drive thirty miles southeast of Eugene, Oregon, to a trailhead on Hardesty Mountain. There are several hiking paths to the top, ranging in length from one mile to six. I choose the shortest, because I will be carrying Jesse's twenty-two pounds on my back. I have not come here to labor, to be reminded of my hustling heart. I have come to watch clouds.

Markers on the logging road tell us when we drive up past 2,500 feet, then 2,750 and 3,000. Around 3,250 the Fiat noses through the first vapors, great wrinkled slabs of clouds that

49

thicken on the windshield. In the back seat Jesse strains against his safety harness, his hands fisted on the window, hungry to get out there into that white stuff. I drive the last few hundred yards to the trailhead with lights on, in case we meet a car groping its way down the mountain.

Beside a wooden sign carved to announce HARDESTY MOUNTAIN TRAIL, I park the Fiat with its muzzle downhill, so we can coast back to the highway after our walk in case the weary machine refuses to start. I lean the backpack against the bumper and guide Jesse's excited feet through the leg-holes, one of his calves in each of my hands. "Wa! Wa!" he cries, and almost tips the pack over into the sorrel dust of the logging road. Shouldering the pack requires acrobatic balancing, to keep him from tumbling out while I snake my arms through the straps. Once safely aloft, assured of a ride, he jounces so hard in the seat that I stagger a few paces with the same drunken uncertainty he shows in his own walking.

Clouds embrace us. Far overhead, between the fretted crowns of the Douglas fir, I see hints of blue. Down here among the roots and matted needles, the air is mist. My beard soon grows damp; beads glisten on my eyelashes. A few yards along the trail a Forest Service board, with miniature roof to protect its messages, informs us we are at 3,600 feet and must hike to 4,237 in order to reach the top of Hardesty. Since I came to see the clouds, not to swim in them, I hope we are able to climb above them into that tantalizing blue.

On my back Jesse carries on a fierce indecipherable oration concerning the wonders of this ghostly forest. Giddy with being outside and aloft, he drums on my head, yanks fistfuls of my hair. Every trunk we pass tempts him more strongly than the apple tree could ever have tempted Eve and Adam. He lurches from side to side, outstretched fingers desperate to feel the bark. I pause at a mammoth stump to let him touch. Viewed up close, the bark looks like a contour map of the Badlands, an eroded landscape where you might expect to uncover fossils. While Jesse traces the awesome ridges and fissures, I squint to read another Forest Service sign. No motorized vehicles, it warns, and no pack animals.

I surely qualify as a pack animal. For long spells in my adult life, while moving house or humping rucksacks onto trains or hauling firewood, I have felt more like a donkey than anything else. I have felt most like a beast of burden when hauling my two children, first Eva and now Jesse. My neck and shoulders never forget their weight from one portage to another. And I realize that carrying Jesse up the mountain to see clouds is a penance as well as a pleasure—penance for the hours I have sat glaring at my typewriter while he scrabbled mewing outside my door, penance for the thousands of things my wife has not been able to do on account of my word mania, penance for all the countless times I have told daughter Eva "no, I can't; I am writing." I know the rangers did not have human beasts in mind when they posted their sign, yet I am content to be a pack animal, saddled with my crowing son.

As I resume walking, I feel a tug. Jesse snaps a chunk of bark from the stump and carries it with him, to examine at leisure. Beneath one of the rare cottonwoods I pick up a leathery golden leaf, which I hand over my shoulder to the baby, who clutches it by the stem and turns it slowly around, tickling his nose with the starpoints. The leaf is a wonder to him, and therefore also to me. Everything he notices, every pebble, every layered slab of bark, is renewed for me. Once I carried Eva outside, in the first spring of her life, and a gust of wind caught her full in the face. She blinked, and then gazed at the invisible breath as if it were a flight of angels streaming past. Holding her in the crook of my arm that day, I rediscovered wind.

Fascinated by his leaf, Jesse snuggles down in the pack and rides quietly. My heart begins to dance faster as the trail zigzags up the mountain through a series of switchbacks. Autumn has

51

been dry in Oregon, so the dirt underfoot is powdery. Someone has been along here inspecting mushrooms. The discarded ones litter the trail like blackening pancakes. Except for the path, worn raw by deer and hikers, the floor of the woods is covered with moss. Fallen wood is soon hidden by the creeping emerald carpet, the land burying its own dead. Limegreen moss clings fuzzily to the upright trunks and dangles in fluffy hanks from limbs, like freshly dyed wool hung out to dry. A wad of it caught in the fist squeezes down to nothing.

A lurch from the backpack tells me that Jesse has spied some new temptation in the forest. Craning around, I see his spidery little hands reaching for the sky. Then I also look up, and notice the shafts of light slanting down through the treetops. The light seems substantial, as if made of glass, like the rays of searchlights that carve up the night sky to celebrate a store's opening or a war's end. "Light," I say to Jesse. "Sunlight. We're almost above the clouds." Wherever the beams strike, they turn cobwebs into jeweled diagrams, bracelet limbs with rhinestones of dew. Cloud vapors turn to smoke.

The blue glimpsed between trees gradually thickens, turns solid, and we emerge onto a treeless stony ridge. Clear sky above, flotillas of clouds below, mountains humping their dark green backs as far as I can see. The sight of so many slick backs arching above the clouds reminds me of watching porpoises from a ship in the Gulf of Mexico. Vapors spiral up and down between cloud layers as if on escalators. Entire continents and hemispheres and galaxies of mist drift by. I sit on the trail with backpack propped against a stone ledge, to watch this migration.

No peace for meditation with an eleven-month-old on your back. An ache in my shoulders signals that Jesse, so near the ground, is leaning out of the pack to capture something. A pebble or beetle to swallow? A stick to gnaw? Moss, it turns out, an emerald hunk of it ripped from the rockface. "Moss," I tell him, as he rotates this treasure about three inches in front of his eyes.

"Here, feel," and I stroke one of his palms across the velvety clump. He tugs the hand free and resumes his private exploration. This independence grows on him these days faster than his hair.

"Clouds," I tell him, pointing out into the gulf of air. Jesse glances up, sees only vagueness where I see a ballet of shapes, and so he resumes his scrutiny of the moss. "Not to eat," I warn him. When I check on him again half a minute later, the moss is half its former size and his lips are powdered with green. Nothing to do but hoist him out of the pack, dig what I can from his mouth, then plop him back in, meanwhile risking spilling both of us down the mountainside. A glance down the dizzying slope reminds me of my wife's warning, that I have no business climbing this mountain alone with a baby. She's right, of course. But guilt, like the grace of God, works in strange ways, and guilt drives me up here among the skittery rocks to watch clouds with my son.

"Let Daddy have it," I say, teasing the hunk of moss from his hand. "Have a stick, pretty stick." While he imprints the stick with the marks of his teeth, four above and two below, I spit on the underside of the moss and glue it back down to the rock. Grow, I urge it. Looking more closely at the rockface, I see that it is crumbling beneath roots and weather, sloughing away like old skin. The entire mountain is migrating, not so swiftly as the clouds, but just as surely, heading grain by grain to the sea.

Jesse seems to have acquired some of the mountain's mass as I stand upright again and hoist his full weight. With the stick he idly swats me on the ear.

The trail carries us through woods again, then up along a ridge to the clearing at the top of Hardesty Mountain. There is no dramatic feeling of expansiveness, as there is on some peaks, because here the view is divvied up into modest sweeps by Douglas firs, cottonwoods, great gangling heaps of briars. The forest has laid siege to the rocky crest, and will abolish the view altogether

53

before Jesse is old enough to carry his own baby up here. For now, by moving from spot to spot on the summit, I can see in all directions. What I see mostly are a few thousand square miles of humpbacked mountains looming through the clouds. Once in Ohio I lived in a valley which the Army Corps of Engineers thought would make a convenient bed for a reservoir. So the Mahoning River was dammed, and as the waters backed up in that valley, covering everything but the highest ridges, drowning my childhood, they looked very much like these clouds poured among the mountains.

"Ba! Ba!" Jesse suddenly bellows, leaping in his saddle like a bronco rider.

Bath, I wonder? Bed? Bottle? Ball? He has been prolific of B-words lately, and their tail-ends are hard to tell apart. Ball, I finally decide, for there at the end of the arrow made by his arm is the moon, a chalky peachpit hanging down near the horizon. "Moon," I say.

"Ba! Ba!" he insists.

Let it stay a ball for awhile, something to play catch with, roll across the linoleum. His sister's first sentence was, "There's the moon." Her second was, "Want it, Daddy." So began her astronomical yearnings, my astronomical failures. She has the itch for space flight in her, my daughter does. Jesse is still too much of a pup for me to say whether he has caught it.

We explore the mountaintop while the ocean of cloud gradually rises. There are charred rings from old campfires. In a sandy patch, red-painted bricks are laid in the shape of a letter A. Not large enough to be visible from airplanes. If Hardesty Mountain were in a story by Hawthorne, of course, I could use the scarlet A to accuse it of some vast geological harlotry. If this were a folklore mountain, I could explain the letter as an alphabetical inscription left by giants. But since this is no literary landscape, I decide that the bricks formed the foundation for some telescope or radio transmitter or other gizmo back in the days when this summit had a lookout tower.

54

Nearby is another remnant from those days, a square plank cover for a cistern. The boards are weathered to a silvery sheen, with rows of rustblackened nailheads marking the joints. Through a square opening at the center of the planks I catch a glint. Water? Still gathering here after all these years? Leaning over the hole, one boot on the brittle planks, I see that the glint is from a tin can. The cistern is choked with trash.

At the very peak, amid a jumble of rocks, we find nine concrete piers that once supported the fire tower. By squatting down beside one of those piers I can rest Jesse's weight on the concrete, and relieve the throb in my neck. I imagine the effort of hauling enough materials up this mountain to build a tower. Surely they used horses, or mules. Not men with backpacks. So what became of the tower when the Forest Service, graduated to spotter planes, no longer needed it? Did they pry out every nail and carry the boards back down again? A glance at the ground between my feet supplies the answer. Wedged among the rocks, where rains cannot wash them away, are chunks of glass, some of them an inch thick. I pick up one that resembles a tongue, about the size for a cocker spaniel. Another one, a wad of convolutions, might be a crystalline brain. Peering up through it at the sun, I see fracture lines and tiny bubbles. Frozen in the seams where one molten layer lapped onto another there are ashes. Of course they didn't dismantle the tower and lug its skeleton down the mountain. They waited for a windless day after a drenching rain and they burned it.

The spectacle fills me: the mountain peak like a great torch, a volcano, the tower heaving on its nine legs, the windows bursting from the heat, tumbling among the rocks, fusing into molten blobs, the glass taking on whatever shape it cooled against.

There should be nails. Looking closer I find them among the shards of glass, sixteen-penny nails mostly, what we called spikes when I was building houses. Each one is somber with rust, but perfectly straight, never having been pried from wood. I think of the men who drove those nails—the way sweat stung in their

55

eyes, the way their forearms clenched with every stroke of the hammer—and I wonder if any of them were still around when the tower burned. The Geological Survey marker, a round lead disk driven into a rock beside one of the piers, is dated 1916. Most likely the tower already stood atop the mountain in that year. Most likely the builders are all dead by now.

So on its last day the Hardesty fire tower became a fire tower in earnest. Yesterday I read that two American physicists shared the Nobel Prize for discovering the background radiation left over from the Big Bang, which set our universe in motion some fifteen billion years ago. Some things last—not forever, of course, but for a long time—things like radiation, like bits of glass. I gather a few of the nails, some lumps of glass, a screw. Stuffing these shreds of evidence in my pocket, I discover the graham cracker in its wrapping of cellophane, and I realize I have not thought of Jesse for some minutes, have forgotten that he is riding me. That can mean only one thing. Sure enough, he is asleep, head scrunched down into the pack. Even while I peek at him over my shoulder he is changing, neurons hooking up secret connections in his brain, calcium swelling his bones as mud gathers in river deltas.

Smell warns me that the clouds have reached us. Looking out, the only peaks I can see are the Three Sisters, each of them a shade over 10,000 feet. Except for those peaks and the rocks where I stand, everything is cotton. There are no more clouds to watch, only Cloud, unanimous whiteness, an utter absence of shape. A panic seizes me—the same panic I used to feel as a child crossing the street when approaching cars seemed to have my name written on their grills. Suddenly the morning's nightmare comes back to me: everything I know is chalked upon a blackboard, and, while I watch, a hand erases every last mark.

Terror drives me down the Hardesty trail, down through vapors that leach color from the ferns, past trees that are dissolving. Stumps and downed logs lose their shape, merge into the clouds.

The last hundred yards of the trail I jog. Yet Jesse never wakes until I haul him out of the pack and wrestle him into the car harness. His bellowing defies the clouds, the creeping emptiness. I bribe him with sips of water, a graham cracker, a song. But nothing comforts him, or comforts me, as we drive down the seven graveled miles of logging road to the highway. There we sink into open space again. The clouds are a featureless gray overhead.

As soon as the wheels are ringing beneath us on the blacktop, Jesse's internal weather shifts, and he begins one of his calm babbling orations, contentedly munching his cracker. The thread of his voice slowly draws me out of the annihilating ocean of whiteness. "Moon," he is piping from the back seat, "moon, moon!"

# FEASTING ON MOUNTAINS

**Y**ou do not want to carry any more gear than necessary up a mountain. If you are Moses, you might haul stone tablets down a mountainside, but you would be several kinds of fool to think of hauling them skyward, with or without the word of God inscribed on them. Mountain walking rewards a person for traveling lightly.

My rucksack weighs twelve ounces. Inside it I stow a windbreaker, a quart of cider, a jonathan apple, and two bagel sandwiches made with cream cheese and pear preserves. In the outer pocket I tuck away a compass, knife, matches, map, and plastic bag for mushrooms. In my jeans I carry a pen and notebook, but no money or keys, since I go where there are neither locks nor stores. Aside from the binoculars dangling around my neck, the heaviest load I carry up the mountainside is my surly mood.

At the beginning of the trail, brain and heart both are crammed with the debris of too much living among people. My mind careens from one human concern to another, from the dangers of plutonium to a leak in the gutter, like a pinball trapped in its labyrinth of posts. Someone in search of a trophy for the bedroom wall has ripped the trailmarker from its place on a tree. So I must rely on map and compass to assure me that this is the path leading up Mount June.

I leave the graveled logging road, duck into the shade of hemlock and Douglas fir. The footing is spongy with moss, needles, the decayed corpses of untold generations of trees. I fill my lungs with the moist out-breathings of plants. Because it is October, there are no flowers blooming. But the rhododendron bushes, with their leaves like floppy ears of donkeys, are a reminder that springs and summers in these Oregon mountains are scarlet with blossoms.

The chill I felt when I first entered the timber shade gradually vanishes as the trail steepens. Gravity begins to define the muscles in my legs. A light sweat dampens my back, where the pack traps the heat inside my flannel shirt. As my body grows heavier with the climbing, my heart grows lighter. Worries dwindle until they rattle about harmlessly in me, like seeds in a year-old gourd. Like seeds they can fatten again, will fatten, once I return to the city. The gutter will still leak when I return, plutonium will continue to cast its deadly spell, no evil will take a vacation for all my striding up Mount June. But for now, every step upward shrinks my cares.

As my eyes adjust to the gloom, I see ferns, shade-loving ivies, and multitudes of mushrooms. Every few paces I find the soil buckled by the creamy snouts. Pulpy as they are, these overnight creatures grow with explosive force. I pluck one, tip it upside down in a rare shaft of sunlight to inspect its flukes. It is a stranger to me—not surprisingly, since I know only a few of the edible varieties and the three deadliest ones. Behind every root, amidst every brown clump of dried needles, mushrooms prod their white or yellow or purple way upward. Some resemble goblets, some look like oatmeal cookies mounted on dowels, still others resemble swollen thumbs. But most of them look like nothing else on heaven or earth except other mushrooms. As I pad forward, not always able to avoid scuffling the fungi into oblivion, I recollect seeing a newspaper photo of a woman holding a basketball-sized mushroom that weighed forty-five pounds. Only in Oregon, land of perpetual rains, could fungi grow large enough to break your neck if they fell on you.

I climb a gentle ridge. The trees pay no attention to the slope, always pointing directly sunward, so that their trunks form acute angles with the soil. I pay close attention to the slope when I come to the first steep pitches. In a few stony places I brace myself with my hands, in case my feet make any unplanned scoots on the gravel. After several hundred feet of the steeper climb, I stop, and feel the pulse hammering in my neck, in my armpits, in my thighs. Breath comes from so deep in my lungs that it dredges up a cough from a month-gone-by cold. After a minute's rest, my heartbeat no longer drowns out the whir of wind in the hemlocks, so I go on.

No people have walked on this trail since the last rain. The only tracks I see are those of a deer. I have worn my reddest flannel shirt, with the freshest colors, to avoid being mistaken for a deer on this Sunday early in hunting season. Color is no protection from the warrior who is bent on shooting anything large that moves. At least by climbing, I persuade myself, I avoid all but the most ambitious hunters.

The first human token I see, a mile in from the logging road, is a sign, riddled with bullet holes, marking the Willamette Divide Trail. Follow it west another two miles, the arrows tell me, and I will come to the peak of Mount June; follow it east and I will come to Hardesty Mountain. The fir to which the sign is nailed drools sap through the bullet holes. Here is a human sign for certain, with its labels imposed on the wordless landscape, and its scars from unaggravated violence. I turn west.

Half a mile farther on I saunter into the open on Sawtooth Ridge, a brown-grassed meadow, ragged with outcroppings of volcanic rock. Here I sit for a spell, chewing on a few dry shafts of grass, sipping a little of the cider. A Steller's Jay, with cocky topknot and iridescent blue body, cries *chook-chook* at me from a nearby fir. When I show no sign of stirring, it cruises out onto the gulf of air and with four lazy wingbeats coasts down into the valley, covering in ten seconds the distance it has taken me forty-five

minutes to climb. Far out over the valley of Junetta Creek, too far
for the binoculars to make much of it, a hawk rides the thermals,
spiraling upward. The sight arouses a deep urge in me, older
than Icarus, for flight. We have soared higher and faster than the
hawk, but have never matched it for grace, for effortless concentration of power. By ingenuity we can fly; but we can never
belong in the air, as the hawk does.

Sawtooth Ridge gives me my first view out over the foothills of
the Willamette River watershed. Some of the land belongs to the
National Forest Service, the rest to private lumber and paper
companies. Huge swaths have been clearcut, and the slash—the
waste wood—lies strewn down the hillsides like gigantic bones
from some battle of dinosaurs. In the older clearcuts I can see a
fuzz of seedlings. They are all Douglas fir, since the other less
profitable species that might grow there have been poisoned.
When they are mature they will not add up to a forest, but to
something like a gargantuan cornfield, with each tree the same
size and shape, placed a scientific distance from its neighbors. As
in any other kind of large-scale farming, the goal of tree farming
is the production of a uniform marketable commodity, with max-
imum short-term profit. Actual forests are ecosystems, thriving
because of their variety, knowing nothing of markets. Wood is a
renewable resource, the lumber industry assures us. Wood may
be; but forests are not renewable, except by forests themselves.

By the time the sweat has dried on me, I am ready to trek on to
the summit of Mount June. A few late butterflies dart ahead of
me across Sawtooth Ridge. They must find slim pickings in this
October meadow. I hear no bees. The only flower I come across is
the scarlet bristle of the Indian paintbrush. But I suspect that a
hundred varieties of wildflowers are seeded down in this
meadow, waiting for spring, and so I make a note to return here
in May.

I soon enter the dense shade again, tramp over soil erupted by
mushrooms. The higher I go, the more great-grandmama fir and

hemlocks I find. Passed over long ago when this mountain was lumbered, some of the trees are seven feet in diameter at the height of my chest. Dead trunks, bare of bark and perforated with woodpecker holes, gleam a ghostly white in the shade. I scoop my hand into one hole, and find a fistful of chips from pine cones shredded by squirrels. A little farther up the trail I watch a black squirrel, perched on a limb, gnaw at a pine cone row by row, as a person would eat an ear of corn. As the squirrel's jaws and forepaws work, scales from the cone dizzy down through the air. From the heap of scales already on the ground, I judge this is a favorite gnawing place.

Walking on into a patch of sunshine, I am arrested by a smell. I close my eyes, breathe deeply. What is it, so sweet and fruity it makes my head swim? I hunt around, but find nothing except ferns, dry grasses, sleepy rhododendron. Then the smell drives me by shortcut directly to childhood, and I am sniffing the pot in which my mother boils strawberries for jam. The vapors rising off the sugar-foamed liquor make my throat ache with hunger. Back again on the Mount June trail, resident in my thirty-two-year-old body, I sniff long and long at this improbable smell. The season is far too late for wild strawberries, or even elderberries or black-berries. Perhaps something nearby is rotting with incredible sweetness. I never discover the source.

As I near the summit the trail levels out, and I begin to catch glimpses of the surrounding mountains. My shirt is soaked again, and my calves remind me that I have climbed about three thousand feet from the logging road. Without the rucksack, and with suitably different clothes, I could be any one of my ancestors, right back to cave days. Here is one of my pleasures in walking: that it has no date marked on it, that it links me with everyone else who has ever climbed up a mountain in order to see. The seeing is the point of the climb, if it has any point.

The trail cuts sharply to my left, and after one last scrubby stand of fir it leads me to the bald rocky summit. My rocketing heart grows quiet within a few seconds, as I turn slowly about. The view is unobstructed through 360 degrees. Patiently, wanting to see everything slowly, I begin with looking at the valleys, where fog still clings. Patches of velvety green along the creek bottoms mark pastures. Higher up in the hills, logging roads mimic the contours of the land. Except for the clearcut swaths, with their bone-white debris and their lighter greens, everything is somber fir-green. Nearby I see the stony snout of Eagle's Rest shoving up through its cloak of trees like a mushroom bursting through the soil. And on the time-scale of earth, these mountains are overnight creatures, mere mushrooms, rising up and wearing away in a twinkling.

Even with binoculars I cannot make out the Coast Range, to the west, from the slate-gray clouds that camp on the horizon. The city of Eugene shows up to the northwest as a copper-colored thickening of the clouds. I do not know which particular poisons lend that copper sheen to the sky. Speculating about it makes me breathe the air of Mount June more deeply. The most heart-lightening view is to the east, where the snow-streaked mountains of the Cascades glisten. Like characters in Dickens, a few of the peaks stand out by their peculiarities: Three-Fingered Jack, The Husband, The Sisters, Broken-Top, Diamond Peak. The rest I cannot name. After a few minutes of studying the map, trying to match labels to visible mountains, I do not even want to name them any more. I fold the map away. The point is to see.

Now the binoculars reward me for my labor of toting them up the mountain. With their aid I can tell whether the faint smears I see on nearby slopes are roads, slash piles, or stone. I can trace the courtly swoop of a pair of hawks. I can gauge how low the snow-line descends on the Cascades. I can detect the blue hump of Lookout Point Lake.

The view is so grand that the Forest Service, in the days before airplanes made firewatching a mechanical business, had a lookout tower up here. All that remains are four concrete piers, each one with a steel angle-iron where a leg of the tower was bolted. Leaning against one of those piers, I imagine the loneliness and serenity a person would feel who spent his or her days up in that tower, with nothing to behold but mountains and sky. There are few other human marks on this rocky summit. A round seal of lead, embedded here by the Geological Survey in 1934, identifies the highest point on Mount June—4,616 feet. Ashes, neatly raked and sprinkled with dirt, show that someone built a fire here—for warmth perhaps, or for a signal, or to satisfy the craving that links fire and mountain peaks far back in our blood.

The only other tokens I find are seven brass casings from 22-caliber rifle cartridges, and one red-jacketed casing from a 12-gauge shotgun shell. Each of the brass cartridges has an F stamped in its base, to identify the manufacturer, and beside the F there is a precise dent from the firing pin. The shotgun casing advertises that it is for duck and pheasant. Beside the words appears a miniature silhouette of a duck, wings spread for landing. The men who lugged their guns all the way to the summit of Mount June probably left home with hopes of killing something. But what death could they have envisioned from up here? And why would they have fired aimlessly into the void? This shooting mystifies me more than the use of trailmarkers for target practice, and troubles me more deeply.

On hands and knees I scramble over the rock, anxious to gather every last cartridge, to clean this place. Stuffed in my rucksack, they will ride down the mountain to puzzle me later.

The sun pretends that it is not October. I take off my shirt to bask in this unlikely heat. The cream cheese oozes from the sliced bagels, and the pear preserves smell warm. With the Barlow knife that belonged to my blacksmithing grandfather, I cut one of the apples in half, core it, then alternate bites of sandwich and apple.

Meanwhile my eyes are also feasting. That is a favorite saying of my mother's: Something-or-other is a feast for the eyes. Like most proverbial sayings, it has been worn slick by too many tongues; and this is because, like most sayings, it names a truth. The truth here is one the mountain reminds me of: I have a hunger for nonhuman spaces, not out of any distaste for humanity, but out of a need to experience my humanness the more vividly by confronting stretches of the earth that my kind has had no part in making. I feast atop Mount June, on a jonathan apple, on vision.

Moses goes up the mountain, because that is where the power is. Satan takes Jesus up onto the mountain, and Mephistopheles takes Faust, because from there all things human appear toylike. Wouldn't you love to lord it over the earth as this mountain does? the tempters ask. Faust cannot resist the offer. But Jesus says, I am not the mountain, its power is not my power. A man or woman is no less toylike for standing up here on Mount June and surveying 8,000 square miles.

One holy book tells us that the mountain came to Mohammed; another tells us that faith can move mountains. I am not persuaded. Nothing but time can move mountains, and that only very slowly. It is because mountains are so indifferent to human pushing and pulling that we use them as metaphors for constancy. To move a mountain by faith would be a greater miracle than to resurrect the dead.

A dark-capped junco chitters as it browses for seeds on the rock. The air is too still to carry tree sounds to me. From time to time I hear the snarl of a chain saw, or a truck laboring up Route 58.

Time ceases to carry me along on its hurtling arrow. Even though the mountains age just as I do, their clocks run so much more slowly that I lose, when I am in them, all sense of time passing. For a spell I feel no guilt about the past, no anxiety about the future. I am delivered fully to the moment, to no-time.

Just as the October sun ignores the season, so it ignores my reverie. Its slanting rays eventually warn me that I must start back down the trail soon if I am to reach the city again before nightfall. The flannel shirt is dry when I button it on. After one last slow pirouette to survey the mountains, I begin my descent. The brass cartridges click in the rucksack, so I stop, wrap them in the windbreaker, then continue down in silence.

# DIGGING LIMESTONE

**S**olid as rock, we say. Build your foundations upon stone, we say. But of course the rocks are not fixed. Waters carve them, winds abrade them, heat and cold fracture them, the twitches of the heaving earth buckle and warp them. The sands on our beaches started out as bits of mountain. The soil that feeds us is laced through and through with the scourings of stones. Right this minute, the oceans are manufacturing the stuff, and so are volcanoes. A cauldron of fresh brew is boiling underneath our feet. The very continents glide about like great rafts, floating on earth's molten mantle, one plate grinding against another, new rocks surging up from trenches in the seabed, old rocks slithering down. A time-lapse film of any landscape, with frames shot once every thousand years or so, would reveal a swarm of changes. From one millennial blink to the next, God would see an altered world. The old Psalmist knew what he was talking about when he said the hills skip like lambs. They do, only we're too quick-eyed to notice.

Still, in our hasty sight the rocks seem fixed. By comparison with our brief lives and fleeting works, they might as well be eternal. Their clocks are running, but only a millionth as fast as ours. There is nothing like geology to take the urgency out of the morning's news. If we could watch events from the rocks' point of view, all of human history, from the stalking of woolly mammoths to the launching of space shuttles, would appear like a blinding flash. Our longest running shows, such as Egypt or China, would be mere buzzings in the ears of stones. Babylon, Rome, New York: snap, crackle, pop. When we disappear, we probably will carry a good many other animals and plants down to extinction with us. But rocks won't keep much record of our brief transit. For all our drilling and blasting, we have barely scratched this stony planet.

If you find comfort in that; if the rush and sizzle of life makes you hunger for durable goods; if your blood pressure goes up and down with the stock market or baseball scores or political polls; if you fret about pulling off the monthly balancing act in your checkbook; if the world has spun you dizzy—you would do well to spend some time in stony country. And no matter how far you roam, you will find few places where the presence of stone is richer than it is in a narrow belt of hills and creekbeds in southern Indiana.

In this region the chief rock is limestone, one of the commonest on earth and the one that wears the shapes of time most handsomely. Like all limestone, this local stuff is a cake of corpses, a hardened graveyard of sea creatures. In the warm, shallow oceans that used to cover the Midwest, invertebrate fauna thrived. As they died, their shells settled to the bottom, where currents slowly wore them to bits and sorted the bits according to size. Chemicals leaching down from the water gradually cemented these scraps of shell together into thick beds, like a giant layer cake. The earth-shrug that heaved up the Appalachian Mountains elevated these beds above sea level, tilting them so that a series of progressively older layers were exposed to the weather and to curious ramblers. If you hike from west to east across southern Indiana, you will traverse belt after belt of limestone, ranging in age from about three hundred to about five hundred million years. There are places where you can leap from one outcropping to another and cross a gulf of a thousand centuries.

My own neighborhood limestone, called Salem, was laid down

roughly 320 million years ago, around the time the sharks were getting their start, a little before the arrival of cockroaches, long before the appearance of anything vaguely resembling a mammal. The Salem outcrop, which extends in a ragged fifteen-mile-wide belt northward from the Ohio River past Bedford and Bloomington, is the largest accessible deposit of premium building stone in the United States, and one of the two or three largest in the world. No matter where you live in America, you are probably within walking distance of a library, bank, factory, church, house, or skyscraper built with Salem limestone. For more than a hundred years now, chunks of southern Indiana have been shipped all over the continent.

Within a few miles of where I sit in Bloomington, there are gaping holes in the earth from which the stone was dug for the Empire State Building, the Pentagon, Rockefeller Center, the National Cathedral, Grand Central Station, San Francisco's City Hall, Chicago's Tribune Tower, the art museum of Dallas and the Metropolitan Museum of New York, Philadelphia's public library and Penn Center, Vanderbilt mansions, fourteen state capitols, and countless other buildings grand or humble. Walk to your town square or to the lawn of the nearest courthouse, and chances are you'll find a war memorial carved from Indiana limestone. In Washington, for example, Abraham Lincoln's statue is surrounded by walls of it, and his weighty words are carved into it. Another limestone memorial you've surely seen, at least in pictures, is the statue of marines hoisting the stars and stripes over Iwo Jima. The Bureau of Internal Revenue toils through its endless piles of forms behind sturdy walls of Salem stone, and so do the Departments of State and Commerce, the U.S. Postal Service, along with many other bureaucracies too numerous and disheartening to mention. Right now, the White House—built of crumbly Virginia sandstone—is being given a face-lift with the palest and finest of Salem.

Over the past century, the destinations for this stone read like a graph of America's growth: first the great international cities, Chicago and Boston and New York; then the muscle cities of the Midwest, Pittsburgh and Cleveland, St. Louis and Indianapolis; now the glittering cities of the Sunbelt. New towers, sheathed with Indiana limestone, are rising today in Miami, Atlanta, New Orleans, Houston, Dallas, Denver. There was a time, back in the heyday of the industry before the Depression, when two-thirds of all the cut stone in America was coming from this little strip of land, an area so small you can hike it from side to side or bicycle it from end to end in a single day.

Digging up that much stone has left a good many holes hereabouts. I never tire of going out to look at these quarries. Some of them are a century old, barely discernible through the vines and trees, as overgrown as the ruins of Mayan temples. Some are brand new. My favorite season for exploring is right now, midsummer, when the tough open-field wildflowers that crowd the stone lips are at their brightest: the intense orange of butterfly weed, the white tracery of Queen Anne's lace, pink everlasting pea, purple joe-pye weed, red clover and bull thistles, violet garden phlox, lavender vetch, blue chicory. They make quite a show at the end of July, a garden no one plants and no one weeds. The high summer sun also deepens the green of the water that fills many of the old quarries. On the topographic maps, these wet holes appear like a scatter of rectangular pits, as if the land had been scarred by smallpox. Following the maps, I hike across green fields and stare over the edge into these green pools, field blurring into quarry. Algae bloom down there like brown clouds, confusing the issue. Sky and underearth meet on this shimmering surface.

Swimmers are lured by the hundreds to these wet quarries, especially in July's dog days. Afraid of stony silence, they come with radios. To domesticate the raw pits, they bring air mattresses, coolers of beer, footballs, sacks of store food; they park their cars and motorcycles and pickups within easy reach, ready for a getaway, like cowboys afraid to lose sight of their horses. They do all they can to turn the quarries into backyard swimming pools. And almost every summer a few of them are hurt or killed. Diving from the ledges, a man cracks his skull on rubble hidden beneath the soupy surface. A girl paddles into the mouth of an underwater cave, and never paddles out. Grabbing a dangling wire, perhaps thinking to swing out over the water and play Jane of the jungle, a woman is electrocuted. A boy, while frog-kicking along the bottom, gets caught in the submerged skeleton of an old derrick. The owners post warnings. The sheriff's men make raids, sometimes arresting the swimmers by dozens; but they do so with half a heart, because most of the sheriff's men, when boys, swam in these same treacherous pits.

The quarries will not be domesticated. They are not backyard pools; they are battlefields. Each quarry is an arena where violent struggles have taken place between machines and planet, between human ingenuity and brute resisting stone, between mind and matter. Waste rock litters the floor and brim like rubble in a bombed city. The ragged pits might have been the basements of vanished skyscrapers. Stones weighing tens of tons lean against one another at precarious angles, as if they have been thrown there by some gigantic strength and have not yet finished falling. Wrecked machinery hulks in the weeds, grimly rusting, the cogs and wheels, twisted rails, battered engine housings, trackless bulldozers and burst boilers like junk from an armored regiment. Everywhere the ledges are scarred from drills, as if from an artillery barrage or machine-gun strafing. Stumbling onto one of these abandoned quarries and gazing at the ruins, you might be left wondering who had won the battle, men or stone.

In a working quarry, where the battle is raging right before your eyes, the outcome is no more certain. The pit is choked with dust and smoke. There is a fearful racket of growling engines, air-hammers, pneumatic drills, men's voices shouting orders, saws

whining, slabs of stone heaving enormously on the cables of derricks. This is no place for the faint of heart. Much as I hate to
portray our dealings with the earth as one of open warfare, I can
think of no more honest way to describe this scene. Quarrying,
like all mining, is brutal. You are ripping into the crust of the
earth, tearing hunks of it loose, and shipping those spoils away.
You cannot do so gently. And who wins the battle? The machinery is very powerful and the men highly skilled, but the limestone resists stubbornly, with its passive weight and also with its
hidden flaws, its fissures and color changes, its mud-filled caverns and pockets of coarse fossils, flaws that render much of the
stone unsellable and so render the labor fruitless, a kind of de-
feat. The quarriers are not often braggarts, as some operators of
heavy machinery tend to be. Their works are mighty by human
reckoning, but measly on a planetary scale. They know that beneath their deepest digging the rock goes down and down, and
that even this unyielding shell is but a thin skin around the
earth's fiery core.

Although the steels are harder now and the motors stronger, the
methods of quarrying have not changed fundamentally since the
nineteenth century. First a promising location must be found.
This is a tricky job, one-third science and two-thirds hunch.
While there is limestone everywhere in this vicinity, it may be
covered beneath too much dirt or lie in beds too thin or suffer too
badly from water damage to be suitable for quarrying. The stone
men look at outcrops and study core drillings; but in the end, like
psychoanalysts probing the unconscious, they have to guess at
what lies hidden underground. Opening a new quarry has always
been a gamble, and one that often fails. Many a man went bank-
rupt from digging in a bad spot.

Once the place is chosen, the overburden of soil and gravel and
weathered rock must be stripped away. In the early days this was
accomplished by pick and shovel, horse-drawn scraper, and an

occasional charge of black powder. But explosives have never been of much use, since they often shatter the underlying stone, thereby spoiling the bed. Human and horse muscle gave way, late in the nineteenth century, to steam-powered shovels and high-pressure water hoses, which have been replaced in turn by bulldozers and back-hoes and dump trucks.

Dealing with the stone itself involves a whole new set of machines. Great mobile engines called channelers, powered by electricity, chug on rails from one side of the bed to the other, chiseling ten-foot-deep slots. Hammering and puffing along, they look and sound and smell like small locomotives. By shifting rails, the quarriers eventually slice the bed into a grid of blocks. The first of these to be removed is called the keyblock, and it always provokes a higher than usual proportion of curses. There is no way to get to the base of this first block to cut it loose, so it must be wedged, hacked, splintered and worried at, until something like a clean hole has been excavated. Men can then climb down and, by drilling holes and driving wedges, split the neighboring block free at its base, undoing in an hour a three-hundred-million-year-old cement job.

If a loosened block is small, it is hoisted out by derrick. If very large (some of them weigh 250 tons), it is first tugged over onto its side, the massive fall cushioned by pillows of loose rock, and then it is split into mill-sized blocks. The flawed stones, not suitable for use at the moment but possibly salvageable in the future, are stacked in piles called grout. The random waste, called spawls, is heaped wherever there's room. The good stones are loaded onto trucks or railcars for hauling to the mill, or stacked beside the hole for seasoning.

Of all the quarrying machines, my favorites are the cranes and derricks. Bulldozers are commonplace. You can see them nosing around any day of the week, in any township. The channelers are unique to the quarries, but they seem plodding, dim-witted, like anything that shuffles back and forth in a rut. The pneumatic drills are versatile but puny, almost comical in their rattling assaults upon the bedrock. They remind me of Joseph Conrad's account of French gunships firing salvos into Africa. Pow, pow, surrender.

No, give me derricks. They are the first things you see as you approach a cluster of quarries, the upright beams thrusting skyward like the masts of a fleet at anchor. Guy wires, slanting down from the tops of these masts to bolts embedded in rock, hold them in place. These webs of cable make me think of carnivals and circuses, as if roustabouts might hang a tent or a Ferris wheel on each of the brawny poles. By means of a boom, which is hinged at the base of the mast and controlled by winches, the derrick can sweep out a circle two hundred feet in diameter and heft forty-ton stones as if they were children's building blocks. After the chisels and drills have finished their brute work, the derricks perform the delicate business of lifting and stacking. They dance the great blocks through the air on hooks and cables, huge boxy fish tugged from antique seas and cast up on dry land. A glimpse of those limestone leviathans sailing through the air on threads of steel is reason enough for admiring derricks.

And so the quarriers work across the bed, wedging and splitting, hoisting and hauling, until an entire layer of stone has been removed. Work then resumes with the channeler; another depth of ten feet or so is carved out, another and another, on down level by level until the usable stone has been exhausted. Since the Salem deposit is typically forty to seventy feet thick, most quarries are between four and seven floors deep. Each floor is marked by a narrow ledge, for on each new level the channeler must start its cut about a foot or two farther in from the existing wall. Chiseled down far enough into the bedrock, these stairstepped walls would draw nearer and nearer to one another and eventually meet. If you greased that abysmal pit, poured it full of plaster, then pulled the hardened plaster out and set it with the point sticking up, you would have a titanic pyramid.

You might well have no use for a pyramid. But the ancient Egyptians did, and they built theirs out of limestone. There's a pyramid under construction right now just south of here, near Oolitic, in the heart of the quarry district. Only two tiers high so far, stalled because the promoters ran out of money, this Indiana pyramid is supposed to be a one-fifth scale model of the one at Cheops. It's part of the Limestone Tourist Center, which also promises a replica of the Great Wall of China. The brochure, written for a swarm of sightseers who never came, sings the praises of Indiana stone: "It's durable, it's beautiful, and it's natural. The material for the ages." Every now and again the national news media pick up this story and have a romp with it: Look at these crazy Hoosiers building the Pyramid! But is it as crazy as building plastic burger-joints in the shape of castles and taco-joints in the shape of haciendas along the highways? And is it half as crazy as building a Pentagon in Washington? If the monument is ever completed at Oolitic, nobody will crawl inside it to plan our extermination. Nobody will demand half our taxes to feed it. No protesters will ever have call to wail or weep or burn themselves on its steps. It seems to me entirely reasonable that people who live near a quarry should decide to raise a pyramid. One is the negative image of the other, the stairstepped pile of stone above ground and the stairstepped hole below.

On my bicycle I follow a truckload of biscuit-colored blocks to Woolery Stone Mill. Jack Rogers, who is the third in a line of fathers and sons to manage the place, shows me around. In his fifties, portly, with thinning brown hair and metal-framed glasses, he is soft-voiced and melancholy and a little hunched in the shoulders, like a discouraged priest. And the mill he shows me through is like a cathedral: vaulted ceiling held up by steel

75

girders, light streaming through high clerestory windows, a nave so long its farther end is vague with dust and distance, and everywhere the cool presence of stone. Leaning in a corner, to complete the effect, is the plaster model of a saint.

"Back in the heyday of limestone, right after the war," says Rogers, "they just kept adding onto this place, building it bigger and bigger. Now, with business so far down, we don't need all the room." So many pews, and a dwindling congregation.

Everything is powdered white from stone dust, as if a fresh snow has fallen. Light slanting through motes in the air appears substantial, like pillars of glass. I worry about the lungs of stone-cutters. Near each work station there is a pot-bellied stove, idle now in summer, but fierce with coal fires in winter. As in most factories, there is a sound of motors keening and belts rumbling. But the ground-note of metal rasping against stone is peculiar to such mills, a watery grating as of creeks over gravel. The smell is also distinctive, calling to mind tidal beaches, damp sand, river deltas.

It is a male preserve. Only men cut the stone, as only men quarry it. In some mills, even the clerks and secretaries are male. No one, including Rogers, can explain to my why this is so. "I guess it's just one of those old-fashioned things," he says. "I've never heard of a woman working in a mill. Never even thought about it before." It's muscular work, but there are women who could handle the machinery as well as the men do. Perhaps those who wrestle with stone imagine it to be female, the flesh of Mother Earth. Or perhaps men keep this work to themselves simply because it is dangerous and dirty. Whatever the reason, the lone female working here at Woolery is the receptionist, and otherwise women appear only in pin-ups tacked to the wall, as passive as the waiting stone.

A quarry block is first trundled under a gang-saw, a set of parallel blades resembling the ones that lumbermen once used for cross-cutting, and here the block is sliced into slabs. The slabs may then be cut to size for lintels or sills or some other use on diamond-tipped circular saws, or they may be shaped into arches and moldings on a planer, or turned into columns on a lathe, or carved into filigree with pneumatic chisels. Traveling cranes, riding I-beams overhead, dandle the pieces from tool to tool.

The machines are built on a scale for giants. The normal-sized men who run them are mostly sons and grandsons of stonecutters. Their ancestors moved into this region from Tennessee and North Carolina and Kentucky, or immigrated here from Italy, from Austria, from Yugoslavia. In the early days the owners sometimes imported foreign workers to break up strikes. Many of these men stayed, joined the union, and went out on strike in their own good time.

"It seems like people in the stone industry never believe they've got a fair contract unless they go out," Rogers explains to me.

The work has always been precarious, boom and bust, nowadays mainly bust, with the building industry sickly. The little building that goes on relies upon steel and concrete instead of stone. Even in fat times the work was never secure. Prosperity enabled the owners to buy improved machines, stronger and faster ones, and each mechanical advance reduced the need for men. The Woolery men look up as we pass by, snap jokes at us, the creases about their eyes white with powdered fossils. They are themselves a vanishing species.

I linger longest beside the cutters and carvers, the aristocrats of the stone trade. They are old men, mostly, with powerful hands and forearms. Working on blocks that have been sawed and planed to the rough dimensions of the job, they carve with airpowered chisels, fashioning gargoyles and ivy, sculpting the statues of a bishop or a rhinoceros. The sound they make is of a hundred ferocious woodpeckers. The dust disguises their clothes and turns them into ghosts. If they were to put down their airhoses and pick up hammers and chisels, they could easily be at

77

work on the Louvre, the Alhambra, or the Parthenon. It is an ancient art, hand and eye coaxing shapes from rocks.

At every stop in our tour through the mill, Rogers brushes his fingers over the stone, a stroke of familiarity and affection, as a farmer might go about patting the beasts in his barn. He touches the pieces of various jobs, identifying them for me: balusters and stair treads for the mansion of a Saudi Arabian prince in Virginia, panels for a Texas bank, foundation blocks for a Philadelphia synagogue, gargoyles and filigree for a college tower in Missouri, an abstract sculpture for an Indiana restaurant.

He also touches the rejected stones. Like a farmer reading the condition of his cows, he can read the faults and strengths of each piece with a quick glance. "These black jagged lines are called crowfeet," he says, fingering a slab in the waste bin. "They'll ruin a stone. And so will these hairline cracks here from cross-bedding, and this change in grain from coarse to fine. The coarsest stuff we call gothic, like this here, with fossils in it as big as dimes, and little air pockets to give it texture. That's my favorite limestone; but you can't sell it to people. They take one look at those shells and get nervous. But it's just as durable as the finest-grained stones."

For my money, I tell him, the bigger the fossils the better. I'd love to have a house molded entirely of fossils, a shell of shells, a skin of bones.

When I leave the mill, he gives me a rectangular slab of the gothic grade, about the size of a bread slice. As soon as I get outside in the sunlight I lay this present on my bicycle seat and bend over to study it. Spirals, webs, curlicues, ringlets: it is a fruitcake of fossils. It is all the shapes of a galaxy shrunken to fit my hand. Comets, meteors. As many creatures went to make up this handful of stone as there are stars in the Milky Way. The rectangle becomes a door: if I stare at it long enough, it will open. If I stare until the mammoth scale of the ordinary lets go its grip on my mind, I will become small enough to swim through these microscopic nebulae.

78

I am still bending over my slice of stone when a Klaxon sounds the end of shift. Men troop past me with lunch pails clunking against their thighs.

"You okay, buddy?" says a nine-fingered sawyer.

"Fine," I answer, just fine, snagged there by the gravity of a handsized galaxy.

Like my mesmerizing gift of stone, the quarries are also doorways, opening down into elemental depths. They seem to inspire elementary passions in people, or to attract people whose primal urges have already been roused. I show you three brief scenes, all from a month's rambles.

A red pickup truck, so heavily loaded that its rear bumper is nearly scraping the ground, backs to the edge of a roadside quarry. Two women hop out and peel a tarp away from the bulging cargo, which appears from where I sit to be a small household's worth of furniture. Judging by their angry conversation while untying the ropes and by their matching cheekbones, the two women are mother and daughter. The older one barks orders, the younger sullenly replies. The mother is about forty, husky, as quick on her feet as a boxer, hair rolled up in a brown beehive. The daughter is in her middle teens, skinny, languid, face shadowed and hair hidden beneath a railroad engineer's cap. When the last rope is undone, the mother seizes a rocking chair and heaves it over the bank of the quarry.

"I'll teach that goddamn son of a bitch!" she yells.

She keeps on yelling about a man whom she never names as she throws stools, lamps, tables, cardboard boxes stuffed with clothes, armload after armload over the side. The stuff lands with a sploosh or a muffled thud, depending on whether it hits water or stone. Every now and again the woman hollers at the girl to help, but the daughter hangs back, hands stuffed in jeans, face tight.

"He can't treat me that way!" shouts the mother. Over goes a small television, the drawers of a rickety dresser, a pair of chrome-bodied kitchen chairs. "Get your hands out of your pockets and *help* me!" she cries as she wrestles with a sofa. The daughter never stirs. The sofa tumbles over anyway, and after it goes a mattress, bedstead, rolled carpet, boots, and a Sears catalogue.

Eventually the truck is empty. The daughter has never budged from her sullen pose. I watch it all from thirty feet away, squatting in the sun beside my parked bicycle, and all the while neither woman takes any notice of me.

Then as she slams the tailgate, the mother glares at me and hollers, "And you can go to hell!"

I sit tight, mum, not wanting to join that other man's household goods down in the bottom of the quarry. The pickup peels gravel as it leaves.

Another evening, and in another quarry, I am sitting on the steps of a caboose. When this pit was yielding up stone, the caboose served as foreman's office. Now it serves me handsomely as a perch, from which I can study the darkness thickening among the limestone ledges. A shadowy figure breaks the skyline and walks past me to the lip of the quarry. It is a man, rather stooped, and he carries something club-shaped in his hand. I can make out nothing more definite in the darkness. There is the click and flare of a lighter. In a moment, whatever the man is grasping becomes a torch. He lifts it up near his eyes, giving me a glimpse of an old man's face, wrinkled as a dried apple, solemn and impassive. Is it a will? I wonder. A marriage license? bundle of bills? love letters? poems? And why has he brought it here, instead of burning it in the fireplace at home or in his driveway? When the flames are guttering down near his fist he drops the torch onto the stone. In a slow shuffle he circles the fire. Once, twice, three times. On each drowsy orbit his cratered face waxes and wanes, moonlike, in the reflected light. It is a primordial dance, a banishing of some evil. Whatever the source of his dread, it requires this stony place for its exorcism. After the last spark winks out, I hear his shuffling steps go by the caboose, almost near enough for me to reach out from my cloak of invisibility and touch him.

In the third and last of these little passion plays, I am planted like a seed in a waterworn cranny high in the wall of a quarry. Of course it is a womb that holds me. But it is also an ancient sea-bed, a good place for sinking down into the depths of the mind. The day is hot, crazy hot. A red-tailed hawk circles in lazy loops overhead, waiting for anything with blood in it to show itself on the rock. An old wooden water tower, held together by rusting steel bands, leaks a constant stream onto the ground nearby. I am reflecting aimlessly on hawk and water and stone when a van pulls up. On the side a desert sunset has been painted in Day-Glo colors. Three men clamber out, all in baseball caps advertising beer, each with a can of beer clamped in his fist, each a bit loose in the joints of the legs. One of them catches my eye in particular, for he is remarkably fat above the waist and scrawny below, like a keg balanced on a sawhorse, and to show off his physique he wears the sort of belly-length T-shirt favored by svelte tailbacks.

This one leads the way to the quarry lip, just around the corner from the niche where I am planted. He jams the beerless hand into his pocket and draws out a revolver. Bam bam bam! He fires down into the water—at no particular target, so far as I can tell from the scatter of splashes. His two buddies also tug handguns from their pockets and begin pumping lead into the green pool. The noise hammers around in the quarry like a maniac in a padded cell. Maybe they are aiming at the fish, which veer in silver bursts, scaly sides catching the light like a slant of wind-driven sleet.

The trio empty their guns, reload and empty them again three times, and on the fourth round they begin firing at the walls. They laugh, hearing the bullets zing and ricochet off the stone. I am not laughing. I have crawled so far back into my cranny that it will take a good lubrication of sweat to get me unstuck. They might kill me by accident. But they might also, I am convinced, kill me on purpose. It would seem more in keeping with their helter-skelter mayhem to shoot me than not to, and nobody would ever know they did it. I keep well hidden. A quarry in a quarry. Except for their laughter, not a sound emerges from their throats. They speak only in bullets.

By and by the shooting stops, the van's motor starts, the tires crunch away. I am a long time in coming forth.

While you read this, new limestone is forming on the seafloor near the Bahamas, grain by grain, corpse by corpse. You could dive down and grab it by the fistful, freshly made. It's also dissolving away right this moment in caverns hidden beneath my feet. As W. H. Auden wrote in a poem about the limestone countryside of his native Yorkshire,

> If it form the one landscape that we the inconstant ones
>   Are consistently homesick for, this is chiefly
> Because it dissolves in water.

Rain and melted snow seek out every fault, scour passage through every fracture, open tunnels and sinkholes, underground rivers and sudden gurgling springs. The waters make it, and waters unmake it.

Wherever holes have been drilled in the quarry ledges, dirt catches and seedlings take root. Eventually these roots will burst the stone. Our roots also go down into rock—the rock of caves, spearheads, knives, the megaliths and cairns and dolmens of our ancestors, the rock of temples and pyramids, gravestones, cathedrals. Entire millennia of human labors are known to us solely through their stone leavings. The only common stuff that rivals it for durability is language, words laid down in books and scrolls like so many fossils. With a touch of mind, the fossil words spring to life; so might the stones, if we look at them aright.

# IN STONE COUNTRY

**E**arth is a ball of rock, soupy in the middle and crusty near the surface. People forget this, living in places where dirt or water or pavement hide the planet under a thick skin. But where the covering is flimsy, and rock noses up through topsoil and shoulders out from the banks of rivers, people remember. They clear stone from their fields, swear at it, pile it up to build houses and fences and banks, carry tales about it on their tongues, bear its weight in their minds.

The presence of stone is unusually strong in a rumpled belt of hills and creekbeds in southern Indiana. Never wider than fifteen miles, about forty miles long, this rag of land has supplied limestone for buildings all across America. I have spent the past year exploring this region, crawling down into quarries, rambling through mills, talking with people. Here are four of my encounters in limestone country.

Near the village of Needmore there is a graveyard atop a knobby hill surrounded on three sides by abandoned quarries. You reach the cemetery on the fourth side along a gravel drive. Raspberries, just coming ripe, lapped against the side of my car as I rolled up to the locked gate one morning late in June. I had the place to myself. From the borders of the cemetery, ox-eye daisies gazed their dark gaze at me. Daylilies burned a fierce orange. Yucca plants lifted their pale flickering blossoms.

I had come here searching for limestone gravemarkers, especially ones that bear the imprint of private feelings. And I was not disappointed. The first headstone I spied was a homemade job carved with unsure hand on a rough slab, for a boy who had died at the age of nine in the last year of World War II. In the upper righthand corner was the inscription ASLEEP IN JESUS, with the J written backwards, the way my six-year-old son used to write it a couple of years ago. In the upper left was a kindergarten sun, light beams radiating out from it in squiggly lines. The picture might have been carved on the wall of a cave fifty thousand years ago, it was so elemental a sign of hope.

I was on my belly in the grass, studying this marker, when a car gritted down the drive and pulled to a stop behind mine. The man who emerged from the cloud of gravel dust was about seventy, a slow-stepper, wearing baggy blue workpants, a white shirt, a ballcap emblazoned with the Goodyear insignia, and sunglasses that turned his eyes into blank windows. His cheek bulged with chewing tobacco and his right front pocket bulged with a revolver. I could see the blond handle, cross-hatched for easy gripping. Was my visitor trying to drum up more business for the graveyard? As he approached, I kept my eye on his right hand.

We exchanged howdies, mine cautious, his cold. He leaned to spit, shifted his chaw, shifted his feet, then just stood there behind the blank windows of his glasses, as if waiting to be told what in the devil a bearded fellow was doing with a camera and a notebook in Hopkins Cemetery at eight o'clock in the morning. So I told him I was hunting limestone.

As soon as that word hit the air, he thawed out. "They ain't nothing much around here *but* limestone." He shoved a hand in his gun pocket and set off talking. He was the caretaker for this place, kept it mowed, kept the plastic flowers in their holders, kept his eye on visitors. The burying plot had been donated to the township by a guy named Hopkins, who sold all the surrounding land to the limestone companies. Quarry holes yawned out there in any direction you cared to look. "There's good stone right under where we're standing. We only dig the graves four feet deep. If we had to go six, we couldn't bury anyone without drills and dynamite." Most all the dead belonged to stone families, whose menfolk worked in the quarries and mills. For markers they favored limestone. "Worked all their lives in it, and now they're buried on top of it and underneath it. Just like a sandwich."

The combination of gun and hand in his pocket still worried me. When he paused to spit, I asked him why he packed it along. "On account of that Leggo boy who's been hiding around this cemetery since he broke out of jail," he answered. "I don't expect he'd shoot me. I been knowing him all his life. But you can't never tell about kids." I'd never heard of the infamous Leggo boy, so the caretaker filled me in on the history. He was a local tough, eighteen or so, who grew up right here in Needmore. Not long ago he broke into an aluminum stamping plant down the road, a brick leviathan of a building that used to be the Furst-Kerber limestone mill. The sheriff caught up with him, put the boy in the Bedford jail. Next visiting hours, Leggo's mother came to see him with a pistol in her purse. The sheriff found the gun, got mad, sent the boy to the state penitentiary for small-timers, up near Indianapolis. Next visiting hours the mother came to see him, and blame if Leggo didn't walk right straight out the door with her, pretending he was just a visitor.

Since the jailbreak, the mother had been making frequent trips down the cemetery drive to leave groceries for young Leggo. "I seen him in the woods and the quarries three or four times, but never close enough to grab. The police had squad cars and a helicopter out here looking for him the day before yesterday, but they never did find him. He could hide in them quarries for ten years and nobody'd ever run him out. There's old guys have *lived* out there, winter and summer, wild as bears."

Pause for a spit. Then: "His old lady give him a gun, of course. But I don't think he'd shoot anybody except the sheriff. You ought to be all right. Just so long as he don't take you for a detective, you don't have to sweat."

When the caretaker was gone I sweated anyway, less on account of June than on account of Leggo. I tried to decide which of the pair sounded like the meaner customer, the jailbird or the mother. I felt like ringing a bell and declaring that I wasn't a detective, that I was neutral in this whole affair. I kept listening for the grit of Mrs. Leggo's tires, for the click of Leggo's gun. Instead, from across the field of quarries, I heard the humph of the aluminum stamping plant, humph humph like an asthmatic dragon.

I browsed among the graves. The ground felt spongy under my boots. Limestone markers from last century lay tumbled, heaved over more likely by frost than by vandals. The names were mostly ones that people around here still wear: Patton, Turpin, Swango, Grayson, Campbell, Holtsclaw, Sears. On the headstone for a child, dead at four, rested a small wooden car. Rain and sun had bleached the wood to the color of ivory. I lifted the car, amazed to find it loose, amazed that no one had stolen it in the years since the child's death. I set it down again, scooted it back and forth to make sure the stiff wheels still rolled.

While I prowled through the cemetery, I imagined Leggo out there hiding in the crevices of stone. There were plenty of crevices to choose from. The quarries to the north were shallow and scrubby, grown up in sycamores and sumac. Immediately to the south opened the vast gulf of the Empire State Building hole. I stood on the lip staring down a hundred feet or so into the green water, and tried to stuff the skyscraper, block by chunky imagined block, into that enormous pit. Think of a domed stadium, squash it into the shape of a box, and you will have some notion of the size of that emptiness. Beyond this gulf the gouges and rubble heaps stretched southward for miles toward Oolitic and Bedford, the largest cluster of building stone quarries in the world. The snort of cranes and the machine-gun rattle of air drills sounded from a working pit down that way.

East of the burying ground there was another sheer drop of ninety feet or so, down to the water of a junk-filled quarry. One glimpse, and I understood the sign I had seen on a hogwire fence when driving up: "Please do not throw trash in the cemetery. There is a dump at the back." Junkyard behind graveyard. Down below, trash spread across the pit like a river delta—car bodies rusted the color of a rooster's crown, bullet-riddled stoves and washers, televisions, buggies, bottles, a jigsaw puzzle of torn plastic. I remembered one of the stories about how Needmore got its name. When the village was still small enough to shout across, a slick visitor from the East was asked what the place needed in order to become a city, a seat of culture. "I never saw a place that needed more," he answered. Needmore still lacked a lot, if you were looking for a city; but at least it was accumulating the debris of civilization.

The height made my legs feel mushy. The ledge under my feet was actually a wall of old quarry blocks, erected here twenty years ago to keep the easternmost graves from slipping over the brink. Some poor souls took the dive before the wall was built. I thought about the old quarriers, working down there in the hole and glancing up one day to see a rain of bones.

The quarry at Romona, on the northern tip of the limestone country, was kept open for a century, from the 1860s until the 1960s. "What finally shut Roll-moany down," according to a farmer I met there picking up stones in a field, "was these two men who owned it died and the widows got so old they didn't know Monday from Sunday. Then one of the widows died and the other went crazy. They had to put her away. And she wasn't hardly out the door before the relatives got to fighting over who owned the place, and next thing you know the lawyers got into it,

and now there it sits, a world of good stone and nobody working it."

Somewhere in his fifties, filling his chocolate-colored T-shirt to
more than capacity, the farmer was a glowering man who gave off
an aroma of bitterness. The field he was standing in had just been
cleared, and the bulldozer he had cleared it with, still ticking
from the effort, hulked there beside him. Stumps and brush and
weather-gray boards were heaped along the edges, ready for
burning. A wagon hitched behind a John Deere tractor was
parked within throwing distance. Every now and again as we
talked he picked up a fist-sized rock from the dirt and heaved it
clattering into the wagon. I had stopped to ask him about the
quarry, whose derricks rose from behind a screen of trees at the
back of his field. Would he mind if I went to have a look at it?

"Damn right, I'd mind. What the hell you want to see it for?"
He squinted at me with eyes like disks punched from a skillet.
"You want to break your legs? You want to break your neck? You
want to get yourself *killed?* God *damn* it all to hell. Every time I
turn around, Honey, there's somebody sneaking back there fishing or hunting or just fucking around. Son of a bitch go in there
and break his neck, and the insurance will ruin you. You ever buy
insurance? It's sky high, Honey, let me tell you."

From all of this I concluded that he owned the land.

"Naw, naw," he said. "This bunch out of Ohio owns it now. All
they use is the gravel. You want to go look at it, you got to get
their say-so."

"In Ohio?"

"Naw. They got an office in Spencer." He chucked a lump of
stone at the wagon. Bang, clatter. "I'm just clearing this field for
them. Get it in corn, put it to use."

I looked at the weathered boards in the burn piles. "What was
here before you cleared it?"

"Bunch of them shacks the quarrymen lived in. Little bitty
things you couldn't swing a cat in. Rat-traps."

I winced. I had missed seeing the old cabins by a few hours. "Did you work in the quarry?" I asked.

"Hell, yes, I worked there. Twelve years, starting in 1948. I was just married, you know, and pissing vinegar for a job. A cousin told me to come out and he could get me on. Shit, I told him, they ain't got any work out there that'll hold me. And shit, Honey, inside a year I was right up at the top, and I stayed there till the quarry shut down."

"At the top? You were ledge foreman?"

"Shit, no. They didn't have sense enough to make me foreman. What I got to the top of was the derricks." It had been his job every week to oil the gears on the hoist engines and the huge black wheels, wide as truck tires, on the stiff-leg derricks. The wheels on the boom he could oil from the ground, but those on top of the mast he had to climb to, a hundred feet up a swaying steel tower. "You talk about fucking *dangerous*. You get on top and the wind's blowing. Nothing to hold on with but one hand, and that's greasier than pig fat. Nobody else but me would do it. I saw an oiler fall once. He screamed all the way down the derrick and six floors down into the quarry. When we picked him up he wasn't anything but a sack of guts."

This led the farmer into a vehement recital of other quarry deaths. "Once this old foreman was standing between two blocks on the grout pile, Honey, and the whole thing shifted, and his bottom half was squashed so thin you could just about see through it." A show of thickness, crusty palms half an inch apart. "We dug him out and drove him to the hospital in Greencastle, him moaning all the way. But he was deader than a hammer when we got there." Another time a drill-runner sat leaning against a tilted block to eat his lunch. "When it fell over, he never knew what hit him. Never drawed a breath or made a peep. Shit, Honey, I'm telling you a quarry's a damn dangerous fucking place."

For half an hour he fumed on about men electrocuted when

machines cut through wires; men smashed by derrick hooks, ground up in gears, scalded in explosions, drowned in trenches, buried under mudslides; men whose hearts burst from lifting or hammering. "They never made a nickel off that hole after all them poor sons of bitches got killed. Even without them widows taking it over and going crazy and all the lawyers fighting over it, the quarry was fucking done for." He swore randomly, cramming his sentences full of angry words. Yet even while swearing, and glaring at me with his skillet-hard eyes, he kept calling me "Honey," the way my Mississippi kinfolks used to do.

I eased him onto the subject of corn, then soil, then fish, hoping he would relent and say I could go on ahead and have a look at the quarry. But when I asked him again, he snarled, "Hell, no. I won't have your blood on my head. First thing I know, Honey, you'd break your damn neck, and there'd be hell to pay with the insurance."

So I left him there in his bulldozed field picking up rocks, which he flung at the wagon with the furious determination of a relief pitcher nursing a one-run lead in the last of the ninth.

Wanting to explore Hunter Valley, a rash of quarries in the heart of the stone belt, I drove out to get a gate key from the owner, Ed Bennett. The Bloomington bypass had carved up the valley, baring prime stone in the roadcuts and scrambling the map, and I was soon lost in a snarl of access roads. I stopped to ask directions at a rickety tarpaper hut that appeared to stay upright by leaning into the wind. Holding five cats on his lap, an old man with a face like a hatchet sat rocking on the front porch between a refrigerator and a cement mixer.

"If I was you I wouldn't have nothing to do with Ed Bennett," he told me. "Go hunt you up a pole cat to talk with before you go talking with Ed Bennett."

"You know him?" I asked.

"He's my cousin. I've been knowing and hating him for eighty years. What do you want him for?"

I said the word, the open sesame for loosening lips in this country.

"Limestone?" he repeated. "I'll tell you about limestone." Then without further provocation he unraveled a yarn from his youth. Sometime in the twenties, when he also was in his twenties, he was driving up to Spencer one Saturday night for a dance at the Union Hall. It was about sundown, and he was all slicked up and primed for pleasure after a week's drudging in the stone mill. And what do you know but halfway there he saw a beautiful girl dressed in a white gown hitchhiking beside the road. Naturally, he picked her up, took her to the dance, and along about midnight proposed to her. She said yes. But first she had to go back home and break the news to her folks. So after the dance he drove her way out in the boondocks, let her out at her place, and promised to come get her the next day. On Sunday morning he drove back to her house. In the daylight it looked all tumbledown. He knocked, and this old fagged-out woman came to the door. He took off his cap and spoke the name of the girl he was supposed to marry. The old woman scratched her chin, thought a minute, and said, "The only place I ever come across that name is on a tombstone out back." Then she took him into the yard and showed him the grave.

"And what do you know, but that girl I waltzed and smooched with had been dead for near a hundred years!" Tying up the knot of his story, he sat rocking in the niche of shadow between the refrigerator and the cement mixer, petting his lapful of cats.

I had been told the story of the lovely hitchhiking ghost before, but never with so much melancholy as this old rambler had squeezed into it. The link with limestone was too faint to make out. I reminded him that I was looking for Ed Bennett.

"What do you want with that old pole cat?" he demanded, as if

91

I had never mentioned the name before. Then he waved me directions with ropy arms.

A quarrier for nearly seventy years, Ed Bennett lived next door to a limestone house, but his own place was frame. He met me at the door in blue workclothes, green suspenders, and beat-up leather boots freckled with red paint. He'd been out cutting grass, and his left hand was bandaged from a run-in with the mower. The top of one ear was scabbed from a recent brush with a fan-belt. When he held out his good mitt for a shake, the lumps and calluses showed that he was not a man to baby his body. He had a good deal of body. His chest and belly formed an unbroken curve that resembled, in profile, the bulge of a nail keg.

Like most of the stone men, Bennett was a little suspicious about why a pointy-headed guy from the university should be so interested in limestone. He lowered himself into an overstuffed chair in his living room and eyed me up and down. There was a magnifying glass on the table beside him and a brass spittoon on the floor. From time to time during our talk he leaned over and let out a spurt of juice. He had additional reasons for being suspicious just now. In the 1970s he had permitted the dumping of some electrical capacitors in one of his quarries, and the fluids leaking from these buried gizmos were poisoning the neighborhood with polychlorinated biphenyls—PCBs, recently added to the Environmental Protection Agency's hit list of deadly chemicals. In the past few months the lawyers and scientists and politicians had pestered him nearly to death.

"I never even *heard* of any PCBs until these letters started coming in the mail." He riffled a stack of envelopes on the side table. "The print's so small you need a glass to read it. How was I to know them electrical things was poisonous? And now they're saying I tried to hide them. I pushed them around with my dozer, sure, but I wasn't trying to cover anything up. I was just smoothing the ground. If I'd wanted to *hide* them, why, in half an hour I'd have buried them so deep nobody'd *ever* find them. But

92

these officials have got to yell about something, and right now they're yelling about a few chemicals in my quarry. If you ask me it's all a bunch of hooey."

As I asked Bennett questions about Hunter Valley, his manner became less defensive, and soon he was peppering me with stories. "The Hunter family they named the place after had a boy called Johnny. Now one time Johnny's Momma got to missing wheat out of her granary. Every day she'd look, there'd be less of it. Where'd it go? They kept watch for rats. But what it turned out to be was, Johnny'd taken him a brace and bit, bored some holes in the floor, and he was draining out the wheat and selling it. Stealing his own Momma's wheat for pocket money. That's the Hunters for you, right down to the ground."

"There was five or six company houses down by Vernia Mill. Some dagos was living there, you know, stonecutters they brought over from Italy. And in Prohibition time they made beer and sold it around. 'Blind tigers,' we called the stuff. You could drink it all night and it wouldn't make you sick. It was that good. The boys would drive their teams and wagons by and load up with that Italian beer. Twenty-five cents a quart. Anywhere you go in those quarries on a Sunday, and there'd be men sitting around with sixteen-gallon kegs and tin cups, and they'd drink till the beer ran out. Then along came Monday, and it was back to work."

A hiss of running water and a clatter of dishes sounded from the kitchen. Bennett gathered a mouthful, spat.

"There was hermits living back in them quarries all during the Depression. Still are today. They get themselves an old sheet of tin for a roof, wrap up in rugs to keep warm. Some of them are barefoot. Never talk to a living soul. The boys put food out for them, like you'd put out food for a dog, and in the winter they leave the stoves burning in the mills to keep the hermits from freezing."

The clatter of dishes rose to a crescendo and then stopped. A white-haired woman—wispy and slim, with the muted prettiness of a figurine from half a century ago—walked in from the kitchen, drying her hands on a tea towel. To Bennett she said, "Do you remember what year the Consolidated Mill burned down?"

"1921," he answered.

"Do you remember what month?"

After a moment's ponder, he said, "July or August."

She smiled, and for a moment there was nothing antique about her prettiness. "It was the last week of July, around noon. I know exactly when it was, because we'd only been married three weeks. I was cooking with Momma, and she and I went outside to look at the fire. I was just sick from thinking of you being down there in it. My uncle was working on the traveler, and my father on the planer. But all I could think about was you."

Having made her personal connection to this history we'd been gabbing about, Mrs. Bennett slipped back into the kitchen.

Talk of the Consolidated Mill reminded Bennett of a photograph I ought to see. Curled and yellow, rolled up like a scroll, it was a two-foot-long panoramic shot of the Consolidated crew, taken sometime back in the teens. Wearing aprons, the mill workers stared out at us from beneath the visors of flat caps. He laid a mashed finger on one of the proud faces. "Just before the mill burned down that poor son of a bitch got caught in a flywheel on the belt drive. Jerked him straight up in the air and there he hung by his suspenders." When Bennett paused, leaving the mill hand dangling by those suspenders, I guessed the story might have a comic ending. But then he continued: "The top of his head was sliced clean off, and his brains was spattered all over the roof. A week later the mill burned down."

"An accident?"

"No accident. But I'm not going to tell you who set the fire. The guy's son lives right down my road. If I'd name names, he'd be up here after me. That's Hunter Valley for you."

Gate key in hand, I went to have a look at Hunter Valley. Half-

Mile Hole, L-Hole, Star Hole. Among the dozens of quarries, the fetchingest by far was one named Crescent. Roughly U-shaped, steep-sided and ten feet deep in water, it might have been landscaped by a Zen gardener. On the first of May the wild cherry trees, gnarled and wind-twisted like bonsai, were in delicate white bloom along the rim and on the blocks that formed chunky islands across this miniature sea. Cedars licked upward like green torches from narrow ledges. On the bank, dogwoods in blossom spread their creamy branches and redbuds simmered with new growth like jets of purple flame.

The quarry brimmed over with birdsong and the rustle of falling water. Cliff swallows cruised above the pool, their call a steady grating sound, like that of pebbles dropping onto tin. After a few swooping runs they glided back to their mud nests on the wall, where chicks waited with open, jabbering mouths. Turkey vultures circled overhead, flattened black V's as in children's drawings. Red-tailed hawks rode the thermals. Here and there springs gushed through cracks in the wall, spreading beneath them a tongue of moss. Near the bulge of the crescent, a creek tumbling over the lip had worn a path down through six feet of clay to bedrock. Snails oozed about on errands beside the creek, leaving slick trails over stone inlaid with fossils of their three-hundred-million-year-old relatives. The black whorls of ancient mollusk shells showed up against the limestone like spiral galaxies. In mud beside the creek, the cylindrical fossils of crinoids lay jumbled with the shell casings of .22 bullets. The skull of a possum rested on the bank with its snout in the water, as if it had taken one last drink and died.

Had the possum sampled the water seeping from Bennett's Quarry, up at the north end of Hunter Valley, it might very well have died from drinking. Among all the PCB dumps in America, the quarry named after Ed Bennett was one of the dirtiest and most dangerous. A year before my first visit, technicians in bubble helmets and breathing gear and snowy protective suits, like astronauts on a hostile planet, had poked around, hauled away a few truckloads of leaking capacitors, filled the hole with fresh dirt, capped it with plastic, fenced it off, planted it with grass, and declared the three-acre site "stable".

The chain-link fence still gleamed in June when I drove out for a look. Topped by three strands of barbed wire, it was the same ominous barrier you will find encircling military bases and nuclear power plants. A man who'd worked on the fencing crew said that, when driving posts, they kept running into buried capacitors, kept moving the fence-line farther out, kept hitting capacitors. Eventually they got fed up and returned to the original boundary. Inside, waist-high grass bristled on the fill-dirt. In all likelihood grass and trees and the skittering insects would inherit this land forever, and the fences would never come down. I had the sense, looking in through the wire grid at this desolate patch of earth, that I was seeing the future. A derelict railroad spur ran along one boundary of the poisoned reservation. Yarrow and multiflora roses flowered between the rotting cross-ties, and wild strawberries were coming ripe. I was tempted, but did not taste these chancy fruits.

In quarries, the puppeteer who makes the stone dance on the cable of a derrick is called a powerman. He sits in a shack of corrugated steel, pulling levers that resemble the emergency brakes on old trucks. In front of him is a nest of gears, like a microscope's view of the works of a watch. Most of the time he can't actually see the stone he's lifting. Instead, he's guided by hand signals from a man who stands on the rim of the quarry. A touch on the helmet means raise the boom; palm out like a policeman—stop; wrist bent down—lower cable; twirling of wrist—rotate mast; palms pressed together—raise boom and lower cable. And so on through a brief lexicon. It's a simple speech, and an exact one. A misunderstanding could ruin a block worth thousands of dollars, a slip of the hand or eye could kill a man.

"If you're looking for an old powerman," I was told repeatedly, "drive out Mt. Carmel Road and see Cedric Walden."

Unsure how far out Mt. Carmel Road to drive, I stopped to ask directions from a boy who stood as if posing for a postcard beside a mailbox, a wand of timothy grass projecting from the gap between his front teeth. "Mr. Walden? Yessir," the boy said, pointing, "he lives right up over that next hill in a little old bitty house, and he's got a horse and a tractor and a motorcycle and a truck and I don't know how many dogs."

The horse, a frisky palomino, snorted and stamped in a muddy lot beside the house. The motorcycle was out of sight, but a vintage tractor and pickup sat in the gravel drive, their color a compromise between red paint and rust. A well-clawed dog cage filled the back of the truck. The house was little bitty, all right, a one-room box of peeling clapboard, with horseshoes nailed over the front door.

Cedric greeted me there under the horseshoes, a mug of coffee in his hand and a grin on his face. "Limestone?" he said. "You better come on along inside. I don't know a whole lot about many things, but I guess I know as much as anybody about getting stone out of the ground."

The room held an iron bed covered with a checkerboard quilt, a television, a vacuum cleaner, two heaped bureaus, two straight-backed chairs, and a wood stove. Because the April morning was chilly, Cedric had allowed himself the luxury of a fire. An open tool box, gleaming with wrenches, rested on the floor beside the bed, and beneath the bed were two scuffed helmets, one for the motorcycle, the other a miner's hat with lamp. "That's for hunting coons at night. You just switch on that light and then you got both hands free for your gun." The guns, three of them, leaned in a corner behind the door. Aside from the Bible, the volumes lined up on the bent-wire TV stand were all *Reader's Digest Condensed Books*. In the hazy windows on the south wall there were two coon-dog trophies. We heard the dogs out back, their voices throaty and melancholy like a nightclub singer's. "Two blue ticks and a black and tan. One of them's still a pup, and another one's no account. But the third one's got a real good nose." The room smelled of pipe tobacco and bachelorhood.

Toothless, lips drawn in as if his mouth were the socket for a third eye, a week's white stubble along his jaw, his face more lined than a roadmap, his body stiff and worn down to a frazzle, Cedric had lived his seventy-one years pretty hard. But he still burned with the high spirits and gumption of a young man. He had bought the motorcycle six years earlier to use for visiting a ladyfriend in Cleveland. "That's ten hours away, and you got to go through cities to get there. Indianapolis, Columbus. I'd never been on my cycle any place bigger than Spencer, so I rode down to Bloomington for a practice, and I was near scared out of my wits by all the traffic. People just drove any old ways. Whizz! But I put my head down and kept riding, and soon I got over it, and I made it to Cleveland all right. I liked it so well I did it five times, and went to Florida too, and on out to California. Only trouble I ever had was I come all the way back from Denver once and had a flat tire three miles from home."

He sat on the edge of the bed, his back as straight as the iron headboard, slicing the air with his left hand as he talked. The right hand, clasping an unlit pipe, lacked an index finger. "A Model-T Ford fell off a jack and cut it clean off." He wore ankle-high boots, unlaced over sockless feet, bib overalls, a faded cotton shirt, and a baseball cap with a picture of a Piper Cub and the inscription: WALDEN'S FLYING SERVICE, HASTINGS, FLORIDA. "My brothers are crop-dusters down there. They made it real good." Cedric's father and grandfathers had worked in the quarries, but his brothers and sisters left the stone belt, and so did four of his five children. One son kept the Walden limestone tradition alive by working in a mill near Bedford.

At fifteen, on the brink of the Depression, Cedric earned his first paycheck at a furniture factory. "Sixteen cents an hour. I thought I'd hit the big money." Even then he wanted to work with stone. But from 1932 until about 1946 there wasn't enough business in the quarries to keep even the veterans busy, and there were no places for new men. When building picked up again after World War II he went to quarrying, and he kept at it for over thirty years, until his retirement in 1978. "I did everything there was to do. Run the channeler, drilled, hooked, stacked. What I did best and longest was run power. It's all done by signs, you know." With hands criss-crossed by scars he ran through the gestures swiftly, like a third-base coach giving signs to a batter. "When you're running power, you can't have a thing else in your mind. You can't go thinking about fishing or women or food. You got to keep your eyes and ears open. The power's got a sound to it. All the wheels and cables, the engine, everything together makes a sound. You get to know how it ought to be, and you can tell pretty quick if it ain't right. Every morning before I started up I'd check over the works. Once I missed seeing a crack in a wheel, and by and by it busted, come a-loose and drove me right back out of the powerhouse. Broke my collarbone and laid open my head."

Another time, when he was working down in the pit, "One of the derrick hooks tore loose from a block and come at me like a bullet. Couldn't duck, couldn't run. Just stood there with my hands up and had that hook beat me on the head. I laid out a week or two after that. When I went back I told the foreman I didn't want to go hooking for a while. I didn't have the nerve to keep near the stone just yet. And if you ain't got your nerve around stone, you ain't much good for nothing."

Now and again government officials would come to advise the quarryworkers about safety. "Half of them never been in a quarry before. They looked at my powerhouse and said, You got to cover up all them gears with boards. Boards! Cover them up! When all that keeps you alive is watching that power work and listening to the sound it makes. Why, cover it up, and you're as good as dead. Some of the owners I've worked for don't know much better than the government inspectors. They're smart, all right, and know how to keep the books. But when they come to sticking their nose in a quarry most of them are lost sheep."

Over the years he had worked in nearly all the quarries in the district. "If things didn't suit me one place, I'd move on to the next. You had to work five years straight for one outfit before you'd get a two-week vacation. There for a long while I never could stay put anywhere long enough to earn me a vacation. I'd get mad and quit and take my lunch bucket someplace else. There's been more than once I've quit one place at eight and been hired on another place by nine o'clock, and my lunch already packed. Anybody'd hire me, because they knew I was good."

Moving about, he once drove down to see how he would like digging limestone in Texas. He didn't like it much. "That stone they've got is so soft, it's about like chalk, and the place where you've got to live if you work in the quarry is right smack dab in the middle of nowhere." After a week of Texas he headed back to Indiana.

On the side he farmed a little, some corn, some alfalfa. "You work a day in the quarry, and you ain't got much juice left to do anything else." In winter, after quarrying finished for the year, sometimes Cedric stayed on to help load blocks out of the stack. But usually he went home and collected unemployment checks. "Most of the boys in the quarry feel the same as me. I like working outside, and I like having my winters to loaf."

His favorite manner of loafing was to chase raccoons through the woods all night behind a brace of good dogs. "When my legs give out and I got to where I couldn't hardly *go* anymore, that's when I bought my horse. Her name's Lady, and ain't she a beauty? I figured I could ride through the woods if I couldn't walk. But them boys I'd go with went chasing coons through places in the pitch dark where I wouldn't go at noonday. *Wild* places. I got to thinking, 'What happens if I fall off way back in there and can't get back on? *Then* what kind of a fix will I be in?' So horse-riding didn't pan out, and I quit hunting. Burned me up. I got one good dog left, but another man runs him."

In winter now, unable to chase raccoons, he watched Indiana University basketball games on television. "I get so worked up, I can't hardly stand it. If you was to see me you'd think I was crazy, the way I carry on, out here all by myself hooting and hollering over a ball game." And in winter he fed the birds. Robins had nested this spring in the toolbox beneath his tractor seat, so he let the tractor sit. When a gust of wind tipped over the nest, he picked up the eggs and replaced them. He was afraid the mother would reject them; but she didn't. And now she would take bread almost straight from his hand. "But she don't give it to the chicks until she's carried it off somewhere in the woods and sniffed it over, to make sure it's all right."

Out front again, he pointed at the huge ash tree next to his drive. "That old boy don't have long to live. It's been struck by lightning three times." Would he cut it down for firewood? "Not me. Nowadays I buy my wood. I can't run a saw, can't hunt, can't hardly get on a horse. Ain't worth a nickel." He cocked a rheumy eye at me to see if I would contradict him. Despite the toothless mouth and the bristle of whiskers and the bib overalls, there was about him the dignified air of a judge. He knew his worth, and didn't need any stranger appraising it for him.

# THE INHERITANCE OF TOOLS

**A**t just about the hour when my father died, soon after dawn one February morning when ice coated the windows like cataracts, I banged my thumb with a hammer. Naturally I swore at the hammer, the reckless thing, and in the moment of swearing I thought of what my father would say: "If you'd try hitting the nail it would go in a whole lot faster. Don't you know your thumb's not as hard as that hammer?" We both were doing carpentry that day, but far apart. He was building cupboards at my brother's place in Oklahoma; I was at home in Indiana putting up a wall in the basement to make a bedroom for my daughter. By the time my mother called with news of his death—the long distance wires whittling her voice until it seemed too thin to bear the weight of what she had to say—my thumb was swollen. A week or so later a white scar in the shape of a crescent moon began to show above the cuticle, and month by month it rose across the pink sky of my thumbnail. It took the better part of a year for the scar to disappear, and every time I noticed it I thought of my father.

The hammer had belonged to him, and to his father before him. The three of us have used it to build houses and barns and chicken coops, to upholster chairs and crack walnuts, to make doll furniture and bookshelves and jewelry boxes. The head is scratched and pockmarked, like an old plowshare that has been working rocky fields, and it gives off the sort of dull sheen you see on fast creek water in the shade. It is a finishing hammer, about the weight of a bread loaf, too light really for framing walls, too heavy for cabinetwork, with a curved claw for pulling nails, a rounded head for pounding, a fluted neck for looks, and a hickory handle for strength.

The present handle is my third one, bought from a lumberyard in Tennessee down the road from where my brother and I were helping my father build his retirement house. I broke the previous one by trying to pull sixteen-penny nails out of floor joists—a foolish thing to do with a finishing hammer, as my father pointed out. "You ever hear of a crowbar?" he said. No telling how many handles he and my grandfather had gone through before me. My grandfather used to cut down hickory trees on his farm, saw them into slabs, cure the planks in his hayloft, and carve handles with a drawknife. The grain in hickory is crooked and knotty, and therefore tough, hard to split, like the grain in the two men who owned this hammer before me.

After proposing marriage to a neighbor girl, my grandfather used this hammer to build a house for his bride on a stretch of river bottom in northern Mississippi. The lumber for the place, like the hickory for the handle, was cut on his own land. By the day of the wedding he had not quite finished the house, and so right after the ceremony he took his wife home and put her to work. My grandmother had worn her Sunday dress for the wedding, with a fringe of lace tacked on around the hem in honor of the occasion. She removed this lace and folded it away before going out to help my grandfather nail siding on the house. "There she was in her good dress," he told me some fifty-odd years after that wedding day, "holding up them long pieces of clapboard while I hammered, and together we got the place covered up before dark." As the family grew to four, six, eight, and eventually thirteen, my grandfather used this hammer to enlarge his house room by room, like a chambered nautilus expanding his shell.

By and by the hammer was passed along to my father. One day he was up on the roof of our pony barn nailing shingles with it, when I stepped out the kitchen door to call him for supper. Before I could yell, something about the sight of him straddling the spine of that roof and swinging the hammer caught my eye and made me hold my tongue. I was five or six years old, and the world's commonplaces were still news to me. He would pull a nail from the pouch at his waist, bring the hammer down, and a moment later the *thunk* of the blow would reach my ears. And that is what had stopped me in my tracks and stilled my tongue, that momentary gap between seeing and hearing the blow. Instead of yelling from the kitchen door, I ran to the barn and climbed two rungs up the ladder—as far as I was allowed to go—and spoke quietly to my father. On our walk to the house he explained that sound takes time to make its way through air. Suddenly the world seemed larger, the air more dense, if sound could be held back like any ordinary traveler.

By the time I started using this hammer, at about the age when I discovered the speed of sound, it already contained houses and mysteries for me. The smooth handle was one my grandfather had made. In those days I needed both hands to swing it. My father would start a nail in a scrap of wood, and I would pound away until I bent it over.

"Looks like you got ahold of some of those rubber nails," he would tell me. "Here, let me see if I can find you some stiff ones." And he would rummage in a drawer until he came up with a fistful of more cooperative nails. "Look at the head," he would tell me. "Don't look at your hands, don't look at the hammer. Just look at the head of that nail and pretty soon you'll learn to hit it square."

Pretty soon I did learn. While he worked in the garage cutting dovetail joints for a drawer or skinning a deer or tuning an engine, I would hammer nails. I made innocent blocks of wood look like porcupines. He did not talk much in the midst of his tools, but he kept up a nearly ceaseless humming, slipping in and out of a dozen tunes in an afternoon, often running back over the same stretch of melody again and again, as if searching for a way out. When the humming did cease, I knew he was faced with a task requiring great delicacy or concentration, and I took care not to distract him.

He kept scraps of wood in a cardboard box—the ends of two-by-fours, slabs of shelving and plywood, odd pieces of molding—and everything in it was fair game. I nailed scraps together to fashion what I called boats or houses, but the results usually bore only faint resemblance to the visions I carried in my head. I would hold up these constructions to show my father, and he would turn them over in his hands admiringly, speculating about what they might be. My cobbled-together guitars might have been alien spaceships, my barns might have been models of Aztec temples, each wooden contraption might have been anything but what I had set out to make.

Now and again I would feel the need to have a chunk of wood shaped or shortened before I riddled it with nails, and I would clamp it in a vice and scrape at it with a handsaw. My father would let me lacerate the board until my arm gave out, and then he would wrap his hand around mine and help me finish the cut, showing me how to use my thumb to guide the blade, how to pull back on the saw to keep it from binding, how to let my shoulder do the work.

"Don't force it," he would say, "just drag it easy and give the teeth a chance to bite."

As the saw teeth bit down the wood released its smell, each kind with its own fragrance, oak or walnut or cherry or pine—usually pine, because it was the softest and the easiest for a child to work. No matter how weathered and gray the board, no matter how warped and cracked, inside there was this smell waiting, as of something freshly baked. I gathered every smidgen of sawdust and stored it away in coffee cans, which I kept in a drawer of the workbench. When I did not feel like hammering nails I would dump my sawdust on the concrete floor of the garage and landscape it into highways and farms and towns, running miniature cars and trucks along miniature roads. Looming as huge as a colossus, my father worked over and around me, now and again bending down to inspect my work, careful not to trample my creations. It was a landscape that smelled dizzyingly of wood. Even after a bath my skin would carry the smell, and so would my father's hair, when he lifted me for a bedtime hug.

I tell these things not only from memory but also from recent observation, because my own son now turns blocks of wood into nailed porcupines, dumps cans full of sawdust at my feet and sculpts highways on the floor. He learns how to swing a hammer from the elbow instead of the wrist, how to lay his thumb beside the blade to guide a saw, how to tap a chisel with a wooden mallet, how to mark a hole with an awl before starting a drill bit. My daughter did the same before him, and even now, on the brink of teenage aloofness, she will occasionally drag out my box of wood scraps and carpenter something. So I have seen my apprenticeship to wood and tools reenacted in each of my children, as my father saw his own apprenticeship renewed in me.

The saw I use belonged to him, as did my level and both of my squares, and all four tools had belonged to his father. The blade of the saw is the bluish color of gun barrels, and the maple handle, dark from the sweat of hands, is inscribed with curving leaf designs. The level is a shaft of walnut two feet long, edged with brass and pierced by three round windows in which air bubbles float in oil-filled tubes of glass. The middle window serves for testing whether a surface is horizontal, the others for testing whether it is plumb or vertical. My grandfather used to carry this level on the gun rack behind the seat in his pickup, and when I rode with him I would turn around to watch the bubbles dance. The larger of the two squares is called a framing square, a flat steel elbow so beat up and tarnished you can barely make out the rows of numbers that show how to figure the cuts on rafters. The smaller one is called a try square, for marking right angles, with a blued steel blade for the shank and a brass-faced block of cherry for the head.

I was taught early on that a saw is not to be used apart from a square: "If you're going to cut a piece of wood," my father insisted, "you owe it to the tree to cut it straight."

Long before studying geometry, I learned there is a mystical virtue in right angles. There is an unspoken morality in seeking the level and the plumb. A house will stand, a table will bear weight, the sides of a box will hold together only if the joints are square and the members upright. When the bubble is lined up between two marks etched in the glass tube of a level, you have aligned yourself with the forces that hold the universe together. When you miter the corners of a picture frame, each angle must be exactly forty-five degrees, as they are in the perfect triangles of Pythagoras, not a degree more or less. Otherwise the frame will hang crookedly, as if ashamed of itself and of its maker. No matter if the joints you are cutting do not show. Even if you are butting two pieces of wood together inside a cabinet, where no one except a wrecking crew will ever see them, you must take pains to insure that the ends are square and the studs are plumb.

I took pains over the wall I was building on the day my father died. Not long after that wall was finished—paneled with tongue-and-groove boards of yellow pine, the nail holes filled with putty and the wood all stained and sealed—I came close to wrecking it one afternoon when my daughter ran howling up the stairs to announce that her gerbils had escaped from their cage and were hiding in my brand-new wall. She could hear them scratching and squeaking behind her bed. Impossible! I said. How on earth could they get inside my drum-tight wall? Through the heating vent, she answered. I went downstairs, pressed my ear to the honey-colored wood, and heard the scritch scritch of tiny feet.

"What can we do?" my daughter wailed. "They'll starve to death, they'll die of thirst, they'll suffocate."

"Hold on," I soothed. "I'll think of something."

107

While I thought and she fretted, the radio on her bedside table delivered us the headlines. Several thousand people had died in a city in India from a poisonous cloud that had leaked overnight from a chemical plant. A nuclear-powered submarine had been launched. Rioting continued in South Africa. An airplane had been hijacked in the Mediterranean. Authorities calculated that several thousand homeless people slept on the streets within sight of the Washington Monument. I felt my usual helplessness in face of all these calamities. But here was my daughter weeping because her gerbils were holed up in a wall. This calamity I could handle.

"Don't worry," I told her. "We'll set food and water by the heating vent and lure them out. And if that doesn't do the trick, I'll tear the wall apart until we find them."

She stopped crying and gazed at me. "You'd really tear it apart? Just for my gerbils? The *wall*"? Astonishment slowed her down only for a second, however, before she ran to the workbench and began tugging at drawers, saying, "Let's see, what'll we need? Crowbar. Hammer. Chisels. I hope we don't have to use them—but just in case."

We didn't need the wrecking tools. I never had to assault my handsome wall, because the gerbils eventually came out to nibble at a dish of popcorn. But for several hours I studied the tongue-and-groove skin I had nailed up on the day of my father's death, considering where to begin prying. There were no gaps in that wall, no crooked joints.

I had botched a great many pieces of wood before I mastered the right angle with a saw, botched even more before I learned to miter a joint. The knowledge of these things resides in my hands and eyes and the webwork of muscles, not in the tools. There are machines for sale—powered miter boxes and radial arm saws, for instance—that will enable any casual soul to cut proper angles in boards. The skill is invested in the gadget instead of the person who uses it, and this is what distinguishes a machine from a tool. If I had to earn my keep by making furniture or building houses,

I suppose I would buy powered saws and pneumatic nailers; the need for speed would drive me to it. But since I carpenter only for my own pleasure or to help neighbors or to remake the house around the ears of my family, I stick with hand tools. Most of the ones I own were given to me by my father, who also taught me how to wield them. The tools in my workbench are a double inheritance, for each hammer and level and saw is wrapped in a cloud of knowing.

All of these tools are a pleasure to look at and to hold. Merchants would never paste NEW NEW NEW! signs on them in stores. Their designs are old because they work, because they serve their purpose well. Like folksongs and aphorisms and the grainy bits of language, these tools have been pared down to essentials. I look at my claw hammer, the distillation of a hundred generations of carpenters, and consider that it holds up well beside those other classics—Greek vases, Gregorian chants, *Don Quixote*, barbed fishhooks, candles, spoons. Knowledge of hammering stretches back to the earliest humans who squatted beside fires chipping flints. Anthropologists have a lovely name for those unworked rocks that served as the earliest hammers. "Dawn stones" they are called. Their only qualification for the work, aside from hardness, is that they fit the hand. Our ancestors used them for grinding corn, tapping awls, smashing bones. From dawn stones to this claw hammer is a great leap in time, but no great distance in design or imagination.

On that iced-over February morning when I smashed my thumb with the hammer, I was down in the basement framing the wall that my daughter's gerbils would later hide in. I was thinking of my father, as I always did whenever I built anything, thinking how he would have gone about the work, hearing in memory what he would have said about the wisdom of hitting the nail instead of my thumb. I had the studs and plates nailed together all square and trim, and was lifting the wall into place when the phone rang upstairs. My wife answered, and in a moment she came to the basement door and called down softly to

109

me. The stillness in her voice made me drop the framed wall and hurry upstairs. She told me my father was dead. Then I heard the details over the phone from my mother. Building a set of cupboards for my brother in Oklahoma, he had knocked off work early the previous afternoon because of cramps in his stomach. Early this morning, on his way into the kitchen of my brother's trailer, maybe going for a glass of water, so early that no one else was awake, he slumped down on the linoleum and his heart quit.

For several hours I paced around inside my house, upstairs and down, in and out of every room, looking for the right door to open and knowing there was no such door. My wife and children followed me and wrapped me in arms and backed away again, circling and staring as if I were on fire. Where was the door, the door, the door? I kept wondering. My smashed thumb turned purple and throbbed, making me furious. I wanted to cut it off and rush outside and scrape away the snow and hack a hole in the frozen earth and bury the shameful thing.

I went down into the basement, opened a drawer in my workbench, and stared at the ranks of chisels and knives. Oiled and sharp, as my father would have kept them, they gleamed at me like teeth. I took up a clasp knife, pried out the longest blade, and tested the edge on the hair of my forearm. A tuft came away cleanly, and I saw my father testing the sharpness of tools on his own skin, the blades of axes and knives and gouges and hoes, saw the red hair shaved off in patches from his arms and the backs of his hands. "That will cut bear," he would say. He never cut a bear with his blades, now my blades, but he cut deer, dirt, wood. I closed the knife and put it away. Then I took up the hammer and went back to work on my daughter's wall, snugging the bottom plate against a chalkline on the floor, shimming the top plate against the joists overhead, plumbing the studs with my level, making sure before I drove the first nail that every line was square and true.

110

# THE MEN WE CARRY
# IN OUR MINDS

**T**his must be a hard time for women," I say to my friend Anneke. "They have so many paths to choose from, and so many voices calling them."

"I think it's a lot harder for men," she replies.

"How do you figure that?"

"The women I know feel excited, innocent, like crusaders in a just cause. The men I know are eaten up with guilt."

We are sitting at the kitchen table drinking sassafras tea, our hands wrapped around the mugs because this April morning is cool and drizzly. "Like a Dutch morning," Anneke told me earlier. She is Dutch herself, a writer and midwife and peacemaker, with the round face and sad eyes of a woman in a Vermeer painting who might be waiting for the rain to stop, for a door to open. She leans over to sniff a sprig of lilac, pale lavender, that rises from a vase of cobalt blue.

"Women feel such pressure to be everything, do everything," I say. "Career, kids, art, politics. Have their babies and get back to the office a week later. It's as if they're trying to overcome a million years' worth of evolution in one lifetime."

"But we help one another. We don't try to lumber on alone, like so many wounded grizzly bears, the way men do." Anneke sips her tea. I gave her the mug with owls on it, for wisdom. "And we have this deep-down sense that we're in the *right*—we've been held back, passed over, used—while men feel they're in the wrong. Men are the ones who've been discredited, who have to search their souls."

I search my soul. I discover guilty feelings aplenty—toward the poor, the Vietnamese, Native Americans, the whales, an endless list of debts—a guilt in each case that is as bright and unambiguous as a neon sign. But toward women I feel something more confused, a snarl of shame, envy, wary tenderness, and amazement. This muddle troubles me. To hide my unease I say, "You're right, it's tough being a man these days."

"Don't laugh." Anneke frowns at me, mournful-eyed, through the sassafras steam. "I wouldn't be a man for anything. It's much easier being the victim. All the victim has to do is break free. The persecutor has to live with his past."

How deep is that past? I find myself wondering after Anneke has left. How much of an inheritance do I have to throw off? Is it just the beliefs I breathed in as a child? Do I have to scour memory back through father and grandfather? Through St. Paul? Beyond Stonehenge and into the twilit caves? I'm convinced the past we must contend with is deeper even than speech. When I think back on my childhood, on how I learned to see men and women, I have a sense of ancient, dizzying depths. The back roads of Tennessee and Ohio where I grew up were probably closer, in their sexual patterns, to the campsites of Stone Age hunters than to the genderless cities of the future into which we are rushing.

The first men, besides my father, I remember seeing were black convicts and white guards, in the cottonfield across the road from our farm on the outskirts of Memphis. I must have been three or four. The prisoners wore dingy gray-and-black zebra suits, heavy as canvas, sodden with sweat. Hatless, stooped, they chopped weeds in the fierce heat, row after row, breathing the acrid dust of boll-weevil poison. The overseers wore dazzling white shirts and broad shadowy hats. The oiled barrels of their shotguns flashed in the sunlight. Their faces in memory are utterly blank. Of course those men, white and black, have become for me an emblem of racial hatred. But they have also come to stand for the twin poles of my early vision of manhood—the brute toiling animal and the boss.

When I was a boy, the men I knew labored with their bodies. They were marginal farmers, just scraping by, or welders, steelworkers, carpenters; they swept floors, dug ditches, mined coal, or drove trucks, their forearms ropy with muscle; they trained horses, stoked furnaces, built tires, stood on assembly lines wrestling parts onto cars and refrigerators. They got up before light, worked all day long whatever the weather, and when they came home at night they looked as though somebody had been whipping them. In the evenings and on weekends they worked on their own places, tilling gardens that were lumpy with clay, fixing broken-down cars, hammering on houses that were always too drafty, too leaky, too small.

The bodies of the men I knew were twisted and maimed in ways visible and invisible. The nails of their hands were black and split, the hands tattooed with scars. Some had lost fingers. Heavy lifting had given many of them finicky backs and guts weak from hernias. Racing against conveyor belts had given them ulcers. Their ankles and knees ached from years of standing on concrete. Anyone who had worked for long around machines was hard of hearing. They squinted, and the skin of their faces was creased like the leather of old work gloves. There were times, studying them, when I dreaded growing up. Most of them coughed, from dust or cigarettes, and most of them drank cheap wine or whiskey, so their eyes looked bloodshot and bruised. The fathers of my friends always seemed older than the mothers. Men wore out sooner. Only women lived into old age.

As a boy I also knew another sort of men, who did not sweat and break down like mules. They were soldiers, and so far as I could tell they scarcely worked at all. During my early school years we lived on a military base, an arsenal in Ohio, and every

113

day I saw GIs in the guardshacks, on the stoops of barracks, at the wheels of olive drab Chevrolets. The chief fact of their lives was boredom. Long after I left the Arsenal I came to recognize the sour smell the soldiers gave off as that of souls in limbo. They were all waiting—for wars, for transfers, for leaves, for promotions, for the end of their hitch—like so many braves waiting for the hunt to begin. Unlike the warriors of older tribes, however, they would have no say about when the battle would start or how it would be waged. Their waiting was broken only when they practiced for war. They fired guns at targets, drove tanks across the churned-up fields of the military reservation, set off bombs in the wrecks of old fighter planes. I knew this was all play. But I also felt certain that when the hour for killing arrived, they would kill. When the real shooting started, many of them would die. This was what soldiers were *for*, just as a hammer was for driving nails.

Warriors and toilers: those seemed, in my boyhood vision, to be the chief destinies for men. They weren't the only destinies, as I learned from having a few male teachers, from reading books, and from watching television. But the men on television—the politicians, the astronauts, the generals, the savvy lawyers, the philosophical doctors, the bosses who gave orders to both soldiers and laborers—seemed as remote and unreal to me as the figures in tapestries. I could no more imagine growing up to become one of these cool, potent creatures than I could imagine becoming a prince.

A nearer and more hopeful example was that of my father, who had escaped from a red-dirt farm to a tire factory, and from the assembly line to the front office. Eventually he dressed in a white shirt and tie. He carried himself as if he had been born to work with his mind. But his body, remembering the earlier years of slogging work, began to give out on him in his fifties, and it quit on him entirely before he turned sixty-five. Even such a partial escape from man's fate as he had accomplished did not seem pos-

114

sible for most of the boys I knew. They joined the Army, stood in line for jobs in the smoky plants, helped build highways. They were bound to work as their fathers had worked, killing themselves or preparing to kill others.

A scholarship enabled me not only to attend college, a rare enough feat in my circle, but even to study in a university meant for the children of the rich. Here I met for the first time young men who had assumed from birth that they would lead lives of comfort and power. And for the first time I met women who told me that men were guilty of having kept all the joys and privileges of the earth for themselves. I was baffled. What privileges? What joys? I thought about the maimed, dismal lives of most of the men back home. What had they stolen from their wives and daughters? The right to go five days a week, twelve months a year, for thirty or forty years to a steel mill or a coal mine? The right to drop bombs and die in war? The right to feel every leak in the roof, every gap in the fence, every cough in the engine, as a wound they must mend? The right to feel, when the lay-off comes or the plant shuts down, not only afraid but ashamed?

I was slow to understand the deep grievances of women. This was because, as a boy, I had envied them. Before college, the only people I had ever known who were interested in art or music or literature, the only ones who read books, the only ones who ever seemed to enjoy a sense of ease and grace were the mothers and daughters. Like the menfolk, they fretted about money, they scrimped and made-do. But, when the pay stopped coming in, they were not the ones who had failed. Nor did they have to go to war, and that seemed to me a blessed fact. By comparison with the narrow, ironclad days of fathers, there was an expansiveness, I thought, in the days of mothers. They went to see neighbors, to shop in town, to run errands at school, at the library, at church. No doubt, had I looked harder at their lives, I would have envied them less. It was not my fate to become a woman, so it was easier for me to see the graces. Few of them held jobs outside the home,

115

and those who did filled thankless roles as clerks and waitresses. I didn't see, then, what a prison a house could be, since houses seemed to me brighter, handsomer places than any factory. I did not realize—because such things were never spoken of—how often women suffered from men's bullying. I did learn about the wretchedness of abandoned wives, single mothers, widows; but I also learned about the wretchedness of lone men. Even then I could see how exhausting it was for a mother to cater all day to the needs of young children. But if I had been asked, as a boy, to choose between tending a baby and tending a machine, I think I would have chosen the baby. (Having now tended both, I know I would choose the baby.)

So I was baffled when the women at college accused me and my sex of having cornered the world's pleasures. I think something like my bafflement has been felt by other boys (and by girls as well) who grew up in dirt-poor farm country, in mining country, in black ghettos, in Hispanic barrios, in the shadows of factories, in Third World nations—any place where the fate of men is as grim and bleak as the fate of women. Toilers and warriors. I realize now how ancient these identities are, how deep the tug they exert on men, the undertow of a thousand generations. The miseries I saw, as a boy, in the lives of nearly all men I continue to see in the lives of many—the body-breaking toil, the tedium, the call to be tough, the humiliating powerlessness, the battle for a living and for territory.

When the women I met at college thought about the joys and privileges of men, they did not carry in their minds the sort of men I had known in my childhood. They thought of their fathers, who were bankers, physicians, architects, stockbrokers, the big wheels of the big cities. These fathers rode the train to work or drove cars that cost more than any of my childhood houses. They were attended from morning to night by female helpers, wives and nurses and secretaries. They were never laid off, never short of cash at month's end, never lined up for welfare. These fathers made decisions that mattered. They ran the world.

The daughters of such men wanted to share in this power, this glory. So did I. They yearned for a say over their future, for jobs worthy of their abilities, for the right to live at peace, unmolested, whole. Yes, I thought, yes yes. The difference between me and these daughters was that they saw me, because of my sex, as destined from birth to become like their fathers, and therefore as an enemy to their desires. But I knew better. I wasn't an enemy, in fact or in feeling. I was an ally. If I had known, then, how to tell them so, would they have believed me? Would they now?

# DEATH GAMES

**H**umans are the last plentiful big prey. You have to be filthy rich, or else live near one of earth's vanishing wild places, to get a shot at grizzlies or tigers or rhinos. But there are people for the killing everywhere you look. You can take your pick of victims—both sexes, all ages, any color of skin, any creed. Choose vicious ones, armed to the teeth, if you have a taste for danger; or pussycat gentle ones, if you prefer not to risk your own neck. In addition to the old-fashioned guns and knives and lengths of pipe, there are dozens of jazzy new weapons available, from lightning-quick poisons to lasers, not to mention bombs, bombs the size of a wallet and bombs fat enough to put a wobble in our orbit. No license is required, although it helps to wear the uniform of an army or the get-up of a guerrilla band. And there is no limit to the number of victims per hunter.

It's hard to escape the feeling, under the barrage of the day's news, that we've declared open season on our own kind. Coups and invasions, border wars and civil wars; execution gangs scouring the countryside, snipers crouched in tenements; explosives delivered by jet and car and parcel post; firing squads and electric chairs; plain old murder in our cities' mean streets: you know the sort of news I mean. We hear so much of it that we forget how odd it is, this epidemic of killing. Chewing on these reports of mayhem with our breakfast cereal, swallowing a bit of the bitterness every day, we gradually stop tasting it. Then a really sour slice of news lands on our plate—depending on the year, the word might come from Auschwitz or Johannesburg, from My Lai or Beirut, from Moscow or New York—and suddenly we gag. Not that, we say, stomachs turning. Lord, lord, not *that*. And for a spell we are baffled by the bloodthirstiness of our species. We are astonished and grieved.

When this aching amazement came over me recently, I couldn't help noticing that all the killers—the heroes wrapped in flags and goons wrapped in straitjackets—are male, and I couldn't help seeing in their murderousness a grown-up version of the violent games we played back in boyhood.

Take the schoolyard, for instance. It was an acre of gravel and grass and weeds, bordered on one side by a farmer's electric cow fence, on the other two sides by the chain-link and barbed wire of a government munitions depot. This was in the country, in Ohio. Behind the farmer's boundary a lumbering bull patrolled, and behind the government's fence cruised guards in olive-drab Chevrolets. At every recess, dividing into tribes, we fought bitterly over that scuffed territory. Within each tribe there was a punching order, from the meanest big lugs down to the scrawniest wimps. The chief bully would bruise the runner-up, and the runner-up would shove the next in line, and so the punishment would cascade down. In nature films I have seen exactly the same thing happen among baboons: the alpha male starts a chain of growling and pushing that passes down through the ranks like a shock wave through a line of railroad cars, and when it reaches the end the puniest baboon, with no other beast to belt, gives a kick at the sand.

Unlike the female baboons, however, who take their lumps and give their lumps right along with the males, the girls rarely took part in our schoolyard bullying. Occasionally a tough sweetie would wallop the daylights out of a pestering boy. "If you don't shut up," she'd cry, "I'll put out your lights! I'll chop you up for stew! I'll move that ugly nose to the back of your head!" And she would bloody the lout. But most of the time the girls stood aside from our battles, mocking us and murmuring mysteriously, their faces like bread dough stretched into smiles, or they rode the swings with bare legs thrust skyward. I always envied them for that aloofness. I still do. To my ignorant eyes they seemed more sensible than we boys, so contained, more confident of who they were and where they stood in the scale of things.

Nor did the girls play with guns. Now and again they would wear fringed skirts or cowboy hats, but they never strapped holsters on their hips, never carried plastic grenades in their lunch buckets, never hid wooden machine guns behind the coal chute for battlefield use during recess. We boys played with all those weapons and more: model tanks, bombers, howitzers, bazookas; rubber knives secreted in our hip pockets, pistols thrust under our belts. Our bedrooms were arsenals. The halls of our houses were awash with imaginary gore. The westerns and war movies that crammed the television after school showed us how it was done, this gleeful killing.

When I was in kindergarten, during the Korean War, you could buy plastic soldiers in the dime store, their bodies molded into fighting position, their chests crisscrossed with ammo belts, their waists bejeweled with grenades. Of course the girls would have nothing to do with them, those mysterious girls, but all the boys played war on the dusty floors of bedrooms and in the dirt of backyards for hours on end, slaughtering Chinese, Japanese, Russians, Germans. I don't think we imagined actual people dying in our blustery assaults—we were too young to know anything about death—but we understood with utmost clarity that the world was divided, as in westerns and GI-sagas, into good guys and bad guys. Our side deserved to live, and the other side to perish. The notion of the perfectly evil enemy hung in our minds like a blank target, waiting for a name to be written across it.

When our own son turned three and got the itch for guns, my wife and I said no. "Why not?" he wanted to know. "Because it

120

isn't healthy," we'd say lamely; "it isn't good for you or for the world." How could we recount for him what we had learned about real cowboys and Indians, about war, about genocide and assassination and the extinction of animals? How could we explain to three-year-old Jesse the sense of betrayal we felt upon discovering that we were condemned to live our adult lives under the tyranny of the trigger?

Unconvinced, Jesse would halt in the aisles of department stores and gaze longingly at water pistols, like a starving bum in a bakery. In the library he would thumb his way through picture books, and when he found soldiers or spacemen he would show them to us triumphantly, as proof that every boy is entitled to bear arms. But we stood firm. No guns. Most of his friends' parents—peacenik holdovers from the Vietnam era like ourselves— also prohibited weapons. No cowboy shoot-em-ups on TV, we declared; no war movies, no cop shows. But here and there a grandparent delivered a six-shooter for Christmas, or an older schoolmate passed along a snapping rifle, or a magazine ad for the Army inspired a yearning for tanks, and suddenly the boys were blasting one another with every pointed object they could find, from rulers to fingers. One day at lunch, still frustrated in his desire for an honest-to-goodness gun, Jesse nibbled his peanut butter sandwich into the shape of a revolver and sprayed us all with bullets.

The mayhem in Vietnam threw toy soldiers and their weapons into stinking disfavor, and for a while they disappeared from the stores. The manufacturers switched over to coochy-coo farm animals and road gangs. But as the gruesome images from Asia have faded, the business in war toys has begun to flourish once again. Now my son is in kindergarten, and all of his buddies keep an army or two in their closets.

"What kinds of stuff do they have?" I ask him.

"All kinds," he says warily, watching my eyes to see if I'll get on my high horse.

"Like what?"

Reassured because I have not growled at him, Jesse bursts into an excited inventory of the GI Joe set, the Star Wars fleets, the Masters of the Universe. "You ought to see them," he concludes passionately, "they're really neat."

This seems like good advice for a behind-the-times dad, so I leave an hour early on my daily run to pick up kids at school and pay a visit to one of the local toy emporiums. Infant amusements are heaped near the door, bright-colored beads and ticking rabbits and jovial pythons. Farther in, the store is divided by sex: girl things to the left, all in soothing pastels; boy things to the right, in lurid shades of flame and bruise and midnight. I make a quick leftward sweep to see what the mysterious females are up to, passing colonies of dolls, meadows of needlework kits, households of dishes and miniature vacuum cleaners. I am stopped in my tracks by a box labeled "Gettin' Pretty," a "Beauty Guide & Cosmetic Boutique" for teaching young girls how to cultivate their charms and give themselves the "high fashion" look. The cutie pictured on the front appears to be about seven; smoothing her wrinkles, she conquers nature's blemishes just in the nick of time. Stunned to find such a relic from what I thought was the dead-and-gone past—as if, in browsing through the tool racks at a hardware store I had discovered a stone ax for sale—I turn this box over and over. A clerk bustles up and tells me that this is only the starter kit. For more advanced cosmetics, I should look farther down the aisle. I drop "Gettin' Pretty" and flee to the other side of the store.

It takes no searching to find the war toys, which occupy more than half of the boys' department. The display for GI Joe ("A Real American Hero") fills both sides of a long aisle all by itself. Unlike the old days before Vietnam put a damper on things, when there was only a single figure called GI Joe, now there are fifteen or so, with a dozen assault vehicles and an armory of battle gear, from jetpacks to cross-country skis. The machinery of destruction and the lingo on the packaging have also been modernized. No more stodgy jeeps and gimpy halftracks. Now you get to choose from mobile missiles, artillery lasers, polar snowscooters, jet-powered helicopters and other whizzbang equipment, all "based on the U.S. Army's top secret weapons system." (Even now the Soviets are most likely smuggling these gizmos back to Moscow and copying the designs.) Collect every machine, the boxes urge us, and use them "to help GI Joe protect democracy from the evil enemy army of COBRA command."

The armies of COBRA, naturally, are also for sale. The molded figures are sinister, their faces masked with goggles or visors or bandannas, their eyes mere slits. ("Why are their faces all covered up?" I ask my son later. "It makes them more scary," he says, "like they're machines, you know, and don't have any hearts in them.") Each of the GI Joe characters has a code name, usually a macho monosyllable such as Grunt, Clutch, Zap, or Hawk; but the COBRA soldiers are all lumped under the single code name of "The Enemy." Whereas every good guy is supplied with a capsule biography, all the bad guys are covered with a blanket description: "Each is chosen for his physical strength and total dedication to evil." No weak adversary here, and no moral complications. Forces of light and forces of darkness. ("Does COBRA sound like the name of any country?" I ask during my son's next playgroup. After a moment's thought, one boy shouts, "China!" and another, "Russia!")

Keeping up with the times, the GI Joe folks include one female figure in their congregation of warriors. At least some things have changed since the Korean War, I reflect hopefully; in the benighted old days, women served only as nurses and captives and booty. Then I flip the box over and discover that her code name is—what? Smack? Fang? No, it's Cover Girl. With that alias, she probably carries a supply of "Gettin' Pretty" cosmetics in her fieldpack. Formerly a high-fashion model in New York and Chicago, now an efficient assassin, "Cover Girl finds that she must work against her beauty to prove herself. She's compelled to learn and master decidely unfeminine disciplines. Her self-assurance and stunning good looks reduce most men to stuttering fools." Reading this account in the toy store aisle, I am reduced to a stuttering fool. I scan the passage again, to make sure I have not made this up. Sure enough, the words are there, describing the same old battlefield beauty, the nurse, the canteen dazzler, the sweetheart in uniform. If Grunt and Zap and the other tough guys have to put up with a female who is intent on proving herself in warfare, at least they can take comfort in her stunning good looks.

A boy of four or so, with a head of milkweed fluff, surprises me while I am clutching Cover Girl. "Look, Mommy," he exclaims, "they even got a lady in the army."

"Sure," the mother replies, "why shouldn't they?" She is carrying a baby on her hip, and wears the harassed look common to all parents who make the mistake of letting themselves be dragged by their children into toy stores. She gives me a suspicious glare. I hang Cover Girl back on the display rack.

"But I bet she doesn't carry a gun," says the boy.

"Of course she does," the mother insists. "Look at the picture."

The boy scrutinizes Cover Girl. "Yeah," he admits. "But she doesn't do any killing."

Exasperated, the mother snaps, "Don't be silly. Women are just as good at killing as men are," and as if to reinforce her point she yanks the complaining boy away by the arm.

In the next aisle I encounter the "Masters of the Universe." These are brawny lugs who are divided, like rival football teams, into groups of "Heroic Warriors" and "Evil Warriors" (labels that the manufacturer claims as trademarks, lest someone else should stumble upon these apt phrases). They are fantasy counterparts to GI Joe, the good guys bearing names such as He-Man ("Most Powerful Man in the Universe"), Man-at-Arms ("Master of Weapons"), and Zodac ("Cosmic Enforcer"); and the bad guys going by such titles as Skeletor ("Lord of Destruction") and Faker ("Evil

124

Robot"). Swollen with muscles, none of the creatures looks particularly human; if you met one on a sidewalk, you would have to scramble into the street in order to squeeze by. One blunt fellow—the "Heroic Human Battering Ram"—appears in fact to be a solid lump of muscle, a sort of Platonic ideal of the weight lifter. But however meaty they may be, the heroes at least have humanoid faces, while the villains wear the faces of bugaboos from the late-late show.

The makers of these cosmic warriors show that they also are up with the times by including two women in their squadron, one for the forces of light, one for the forces of darkness. Like Cover Girl they are not only tough customers; they are also curvaceous charmers, doubtless capable of reducing the muscle-bound he-men to stuttering fools when the need arises. Rigged out in high-heeled boots, tiaras, and body suits that elevate their breasts and bare their haunchy hips, looking in fact like professional cheerleaders (who are dressed to look like hookers), these dangerous ladies are sorceresses who fight with magic instead of swords.

Beyond the Masters of the Universe I spy other galactic armies, battalion after battalion, with exotic weapons stacked in boxes to the ceiling and names drawn from the most recent outerspace slam-bang movies. But my eyes are beginning to glaze over. I retreat from the aisles of bruise-and-flame-colored toys, past the "Screaming Eagles" combat set, past electronic machine guns and laser pistols, past falcon-faced missiles and alien bombers. After so many futuristic weapons, it is almost touching to glimpse, as I hurry out, a flintlock pistol with coonskin hat, a cowboy-and-Indian set called Fort Courage, and a Lone-Ranger outfit complete with six-shooter, mask, and silver bullets.

My son is intrigued, when I explain why I am a few minutes late in picking him up from kindergarten, to learn that I took his advice and went browsing among the war toys. Imagine that— old curmudgeonly Dad, who won't allow so much as a popgun into the house, out at the mall studying lasers and assassins. Jesse hopes for a miraculous conversion, for Dad to see the light and agree to arm the household.

"What do you think?" he asks cautiously.

"They're interesting," I answer vaguely.

"Did you like them?"

"I'm not sure."

"*I* think they're really *nifty*," he cries, his wariness overwhelmed by his enthusiasm, "especially GI Joe. Just about the neatest thing there is."

"What's so nifty about them?" I ask him.

"There's all the soldiers, bunches of them, and all the stuff that goes with them, the backpacks and skis. And vehicles! Every kind you can imagine."

"You could have the same stuff with campers or forest rangers. Why not a set of mountain climbers?"

"But GI Joe's got planes, you know, and rockets, and rifles and . . ." He checks himself, mindful of the family taboo on guns. "And there's COBRA. You know—the enemy."

"Yeah, I saw them. Why are they enemies?"

"They just *are*. I don't know. They're bad. They're against GI Joe."

"So that makes it more fun, having an enemy?"

He shrugs. "It's the only way you can have a war."

We stop on our way home to buy milk at the supermarket. Waiting in the checkout line, I notice the headlines on one of the weekly scandal sheets: SECRET SAFARIS PREY ON POOR VILLAGERS. RICH HUNTERS KILL HUMANS FOR SPORT. FAT-CAT SPORTSMEN SHOOT CHILDREN LIKE RABBITS IN WILDS OF INDIA.

"What's that about?" says Jesse.

"Oh," I mutter, "just a story."

Unsatisfied, suspicious of a parental cover-up, he puts his brand new reading skills to use, stumbling over the bulky words. "Poor," he says. "Rich . . . fat . . . cat," and then he manages to sound out "shoot . . . children . . . like . . . rabbits." He repeats the phrase quizzically. "Shoot children like rabbits? What are they *talking* about?"

"It's just a made-up story," I assure him. Turn his attention elsewhere, I think. But there is nothing in sight except cigarettes, candy, horoscopes, and glamour magazines featuring scrawny models in unbuttoned dresses. As I pay for the milk, I grump at the cashier, "Why do you jam all this trash up here where we have to stand in line and look at it?" The clerk, a high-school boy wearing a clown's polka-dot bowtie and a have-a-happy-day button, blinks at me in consternation.

In the parking lot I tell Jesse, "People think up silly things like that to sell papers and magazines. Nobody's hunting children, believe me." But I'm not so sure what to believe myself, and I suspect that Jesse has already planted this bit of news in the patch of his child's memory devoted to dread, another seed of nightmare.

We find our car flanked by two pickups, each with a rifle in the gun rack of the cab window. Back when I worked as a carpenter in the Vietnam era, the builder I rode with carried a framing level on his rack. The other guys in our crew—bearded, ponytailed, lanky young galoots who talked politics and karma while they hammered—displayed umbrellas or walking sticks in their trucks. But nowadays, here in southern Indiana, half the gun racks I see are loaded.

"Why do they need those rifles?" Jesse asks, not for the first time. He can't understand why his mom and dad forbid him to own so much as a cap pistol when all these grown men are hauling arsenals around in their pickups.

I remember putting the same question to a fellow who was sharing a gas pump with me some time ago. While the two of us waited for our tanks to fill, I nodded at the rear window of his truck and asked, in a cordial way, why he carried three rifles. Just as cordially, he replied, "The twenty-two is for varmints, the twelve-gauge is for deer, and the thirty-ought-six is for people who mess with me." He had a fat, cherubic face, like an aging choirboy, and smiled as he spoke.

Not long after this gas-station chat, when a man pulled up at a stop sign near our house, three boys hiding in the bushes peppered his truck with kernels of field corn, a traditional Halloween stunt. Instead of laughing, the man grabbed a shotgun from the rack behind his head and fired blindly into the bushes, putting two of the boys in the hospital.

"They don't really *need* those guns," I tell Jesse, not for the first time. "It isn't as if they have to protect their lambs from mountain lions, or fight off highwaymen."

"I guess they just like having them up there to look at," says Jesse. "It kind of makes them feel good, you know. Like hanging pictures on the wall."

As we drive home, he turns around several times, studying our rear window. I imagine he is wondering if you can buy gun racks for compact station wagons.

Wherever it comes from—genes or movies, phallic fixation or the breeze—this hankering for guns seems to be as potent in young boys as the hankering for sex will be later on. The trouble, of course, is that too many boys refuse to surrender their six-shooters when their beards grow in. They trade in the toys for the real thing.

A lawyer I know owns a collection of machine guns, for which he has secured a special license. He's a neighborly sort of guy, who carries jumper-cables in his trunk and helps folks start their cars on winter mornings. He looks in regularly on an eightyish man who lives alone next door. He raises herbs in a backyard garden and shares them up and down the street.

"What do you want with machine guns?" I ask him.

"They're a good investment," he claims.

But every weekend he takes one of his gleaming investments to the firing range and burns up ammo worth more than any profit he's likely to make from selling his collection.

The firing range is crowded with shooters, and so is the countryside. Any day I'm feeling reckless I can take a hike in the hills south of town and hear gunfire, or I can watch marksmen blast floating junk in the abandoned limestone quarries. I find perforated cans squatting on stumps, and the shattered necks of bottles hanging by string from branches. On the ground, shell casings are scattered more thickly than hickory nuts. Here and there an abandoned car lies riddled and rusting in the ditch. Every road sign leaks daylight through bullet holes. It's as if private militias were constantly training in the woods.

There are sixty million or so handguns in our country, little packages of annihilation within arm's reach, about one for every four of us. Two or three million new ones are sold each year. You can get a license to manufacture them for fifty bucks, and for ten bucks you can get a license to sell them. Unlike rifles, which hunters use as an excuse for hiking in the woods, handguns are worthless for hunting and next to worthless for target shooting. About all they are good for is putting large holes in people at close range, and for that they are very good. In recent years, handguns have been used in killing some twenty-five thousand people a year in the U.S., including murders, suicides, and accidents. Knowing these numbers, when I am in crowds I don't worry about what other folks might pick from my pocket; I worry about what they might pluck from their own.

To judge from interviews on television, every third house or so has a basement stocked with two years' worth of food and a bedroom crammed with artillery. "We aim to survive," a grim-faced man announces to the camera. The barrels of guns, row upon row, gleam from the wall behind him. His son, a gap-toothed smiler about the age of Jesse, shows how to dismantle and reassemble a submachine gun. His wife holds up a jar of pickled beets for inspection. "Survive what?" the interviewer asks. "Everything," the father declares, flinging his arms wide, "the whole mess. When it all comes apart, we're going to sit right here and stay alive."

At the newsstand I discover *Survival* magazine, aimed at those who are larding their basements with pickled beets and submachine guns. I browse through other magazines with titles such as *Knife Journal* ("How to Start Your Sword Collection"), *Shooting, Safari* ("Bagging a Pronghorn Despite the Ban"), *American Hunter, American Rifleman, American Handgunner, Guns & Ammo* ("The Most Powerful Rifle in the World"), and plain old *Guns*.

The most chilling selection at the newsstand is *Soldier of Fortune*, "The Journal for Professional Adventurers." When I buy a copy I ask the drowsy salesgirl to put it in a sack for me. This provokes a tilted smile from her. "Enjoy your reading," she says. From the cover, which shows U.S. Marines in battle gear landing on Grenada, through the articles about military hardware and bombing raids and Central American gun-running, to the classified ads for mercenaries and bounty hunters, the magazine is an exaltation of violence. It is a grown-up's version of GI Joe, complete with high-tech weapons, page after page of survival gear (bullet-proof vests and $300 knives), big-bosomed ladies for distracting the troops and for selling products, and a division of the world between Heroic Warriors (U.S. soldiers and our client armies) and Evil Warriors (Soviet soldiers and *their* clients). The ads offer Nazi hats and kamikaze headbands, instructions for making napalm or for evading lie-detector tests, ballpoint pens that convert into stilettos, "Viet Cong Hunting Club" badges that show a guerrilla caught in the cross-hairs of a gunsight, or human skulls pierced by twelve-inch daggers. "Genuine Human skull (not plastic) zapped by USMC combat knife," the ad promises. "Unique Bizarre trophy for your den or gunroom . . . mind-boggling!" The lily-livered pacifists, whose minds really do boggle at all this bloody-mindedness, are in fact (as one essay observes) "on the *other side*—they are fighting the war, just as surely as a left-wing lobbyist in Washington or a . . . guerrilla in the bush." The other side, of course, belongs to COBRA, Satan, the evil warriors, the Commies, the perennial brutes in black hats.

Mystified and more than a little scared by this civilian arms race, I stop by a local gun shop to see what's for sale. The downstairs is heaped with clothes. The weapons are on the second floor. At the top of the stairs a noose dangles down— "RESERVED FOR SHOPLIFTERS"—and on the wall beside it is a plaque inscribed with the second article of the Bill of Rights, guaranteeing us all the freedom to bear arms.

Except for some tents and fishing tackle, the whole of this second floor is devoted to helping us fulfill our constitutional privilege: there are enough crossbows, rifles, knives, revolvers, and shotguns to equip most of the able-bodied folks in town. It is a candy store for gun lovers, case after case of gleaming weapons. In the faces of men who are gazing at the wares, there is a child's or a lover's undisguised hunger. One man in a three-piece suit actually presses his nose to the glass, the better to study a selection of pistols. Another fellow, who has been handed a thirty-thirty for inspection, strokes the barrel and the satiny walnut stock with his eyes closed.

The stuffed heads of deer, bear, mountain goat, and moose peer down solemnly from the walls, their glass eyes glinting. Lesser beasts are represented by entire carcasses, including a turkey, a mallard, and a swordfish. Skins of fox and raccoon hang from nails. All these moldering trophies remind me of the prize teddy bears at shooting galleries. "Win one for your tootsie!" the barker would cry. "Five shots for a quarter!" Beside a shelf stacked with brochures from the National Rifle Association, a sheet of tin is on display, decorated with bullet holes that trace out the profile of an Indian in feathered headdress and signed by one Tom Frye, Remington Arms Co., 1971. I sit for awhile in a chair fashioned from a barrel and leaf through gun catalogs. The cover of the one for Winchester Sporting Arms shows John Wayne in cowboy get-up, his eyes fixed on the horizon, the air aswirl with smoke, and the sky blotted out by the Stars and Stripes.

At one end of this armory, set off by a split-rail fence and gate, there is a museum of hunting and military paraphernalia. The white-haired clerk who keeps watch nearby tells me, "Go right on in," and I thank him and do. Bayonets, mess-kits, medals, cartridge-belts, daggers, photographs of big game hunters kneeling beside deflated elephants and spread-eagled tigers: surrounded by these mementos of mayhem, I begin to feel the panicky smothering sensation that drove me from the toy store. Through a doorway that opens beyond this little museum into an inner sanctum, I glimpse the snowy pelt of a polar bear spread on the floor and the horns of a buffalo curling above the store-keeper's desk. Turning away, I imagine a succession of rooms opening beyond that one, gallery after gallery of corpses.

So where does the desire come from, this boy's compulsion to play at killing, this man's compulsion to kill for real? Pick your own answer. Original sin, the old mark of Cain, says a theologian. Too much testosterone, explains a biologist. Territorial imperative, insists an anthropologist. The will to power or the lust for death, say opposing psychologists. A historian assures us that it is all a legacy of life on the frontier. A feminist attributes it to male insecurity and the desire for sexual dominance. No, no, other pundits declare: it's television; it's food additives; it's the animal id.

"I just think playing with guns and soldiers is *fun*," says Jesse, and said the boy in me. Troubled about all this because *I* am troubled, he asks me, "What's so bad about playing war? It's all just pretend."

It *is* pretend when it starts, this toying with murder, and for most of us it remains make-believe. I swaggered around at cowboys-and-Indians, waddled about with six-shooters, shot up enemy armies, longed for and finally got my own BB gun and .22. Most of the men I knew in my childhood were hunters. Few things in life have given me more pleasure than tramping through the leafruck and dry grasses of October beside my father, on the lookout for anything covered in feathers or fur. And yet here I sit, fearing and hating every manner of weapon. If all the world's soldiers handed in their dog tags and uniforms tomorrow, I would dance with giddy pleasure.

Many of my old playmates, those boyhood soldiers, probably feel the same. If their trigger-fingers start itching, they content themselves with blasting aliens in a video arcade, or hunting rabbits and deer on weekends. But on the day of my graduation from high school, seven of my buddies drove to Cleveland to get themselves tattoos; on the next day, wanting to handle real guns, they all joined the Marines. I met another one of those playmates years later, in England, where he was resting up at a U.S. air base before returning to Vietnam for another bout of bombing. "It's beautiful," he said, describing night raids over Hanoi, "to see those fires blooming down there like flowers and to feel this whacking great machine turn in your hands." War is hell, say the generals; but it is also heaven, say many veterans. Remembering combat, ex-warriors will tell you they have never been so alive, never so happy, since the shooting stopped.

Soldiers or not, we veterans of childhood wars carry in our innermost ears the growl of machine guns, remember in our muscles the jab of a bayonet, preserve the star-image of bursting bombs. We know all about enemies. We understand how to divide the universe into the forces of light and the forces of darkness. On the edge of sleep, our hands curl and our fingers twitch. Massacres wait in us, like the lines of plays we rehearsed long ago. If we don't enact them ourselves, we feel little surprise when someone else does. Bang, bang, you're dead, we sing inwardly. And somebody really dies.

133

# DOING TIME
# IN THE THIRTEENTH CHAIR

**T**he courtroom is filled with the ticking of a clock and the smell of mold. Listening to the minutes click away, I imagine bombs or mechanical hearts sealed behind the limestone walls. Forty of us have been yanked out of our usual orbits and called to appear for jury duty in this ominous room, beneath the stained-glass dome of the county courthouse. We sit in rows like strangers in a theater, coats rumpled in our laps, crossing and uncrossing our legs, waiting for the show to start.

I feel sulky and rebellious, the way I used to feel when a grade-school teacher made me stay inside during recess. This was supposed to have been the first day of my Christmas vacation, and the plain, uncitizenly fact is that I don't want to be here. I want to be home hammering together some bookshelves for my wife. I want to be out tromping the shores of Lake Monroe with my eye cocked skyward for bald eagles and sharp-shinned hawks.

But the computer-printed letter said to report today for jury duty, and so here I sit. The judge beams down at us from his bench. Tortoise-shell glasses, twenty-dollar haircut, square boyish face: although probably in his early forties, he could pass for a student-body president. He reminds me of an owlish television know-it-all named Mr. Wizard who used to conduct scientific experiments (Magnetism! Litmus tests! Sulphur dioxide!) on a kids' show in the 1950s. Like Mr. Wizard, he lectures us in slow, pe-

dantic speech: trial by one's peers, tradition stretching back centuries to England, defendant innocent until proven guilty beyond
a reasonable doubt, and so abundantly on. I spy around for the
clock. It must be overhead, I figure, up in the cupola above the
dome, raining its ticktocks down on us.

When the lecture is finished, the judge orders us to rise, lift
our hands, and swear to uphold the truth. There is a cracking of
winter-stiff knees as we stand and again as we sit down. Then he
introduces the principal actors: the sleek young prosecutor, who
peacocks around like a politician on the hustings; the married
pair of brooding, elegantly dressed defense lawyers; and the
defendant. I don't want to look at this man who is charged with
crimes against the "peace and dignity" of the State of Indiana. I
don't want anything to do with his troubles. But I grab an image
anyway, of a squat, slit-eyed man about my age, mid-thirties,
stringy black hair parted in the middle and dangling like curtains
across his face, sparse black beard. The chin whiskers and
squinted-up eyes make him look faintly Chinese, and faintly
grimacing.

Next the judge reads a list of twelve names, none of them
mine, and twelve sworn citizens shuffle into the jury box. The
lawyers have at them, darting questions. How do you feel about
drugs? Would you say the defendant there looks guilty because
he has a beard? Are you related to any police officers? Are you
pregnant? When these twelve have finished answering, the attorneys scribble names on sheets of paper which they hand to the
judge, and eight of the first bunch are sent packing. The judge
reads eight more names, the jury box fills up with fresh bodies,
the questioning resumes. Six of these get the heave-ho. And so
the lawyers cull through the potential jurors, testing and chuck-
ing them like two men picking over apples in the supermarket.
At length they agree on a dozen, and still my name has not been
called. Hooray, I think. I can build those bookshelves after all,
can watch those hawks.

Before setting the rest of us free, however, the judge consults his list. "I am calling alternate juror number one," he says, and then he pronounces my name.

Groans echo down my inmost corridors. For the first time I notice a thirteenth chair beside the jury box, and that is where the judge orders me to go.

"Yours is the most frustrating job," the judge advises me soothingly. "Unless someone else falls ill or gets called away, you will have to listen to all the proceedings without taking part in the jury's final deliberations or decisions."

I feel as though I have been invited to watch the first four acts of a five-act play. Never mind, I console myself: the lawyers will throw me out. I'm the only one in the courtroom besides the defendant who sports a beard or long hair. A backpack decorated with NO NUKES and PEACE NOW and SAVE THE WHALES buttons leans against my boots. How can they expect me, a fiction writer, to confine myself to facts? I am unreliable, a confessed fabulist, a marginal Quaker and Wobbly socialist, a man so out of phase with my community that I am thrown into fits of rage by the local newspaper. The lawyers will take a good look at me and race one another to the bench for the privilege of having the judge boot me out.

But neither Mr. Defense nor Mr. Prosecution quite brings himself to focus on my shady features. Each asks me a perfunctory question, the way vacationers will press a casual thumb against the spare tire before hopping into the car for a trip. If there's air in the tire, you don't bother about blemishes. And that is all I am, a spare juror stashed away in the trunk of the court, in case one of the twelve originals gives out during the trial.

Ticktock. The judge assures us that we should be finished in five days, just in time for Christmas. The real jurors exchange forlorn glances. Here I sit, number thirteen, and nobody looks my way. Knowing I am stuck here for the duration, I perk up,

136

blink my eyes. Like the bear going over the mountain, I might as well see what I can see.

What I see is a parade of mangled souls. Some of them sit on the witness stand and reveal their wounds; some of them remain off-stage, summoned up only by the words of those who testify. The case has to do with the alleged sale, earlier this year, of hashish and cocaine to a confidential informer. First the prosecutor stands at a podium in front of the jury and tells us how it all happened, detail by criminal detail, and promises to prove every fact to our utter satisfaction. Next, one of the defense attorneys has a fling at us. It is the husband of the Mr.-and-Mrs. team, a melancholy-looking man with bald pate and mutton-chop side-burns, deep creases in the chocolate skin of his forehead. Lean-ing on the podium, he vows that he will raise a flock of doubts in our minds—grave doubts, reasonable doubts—particularly re-garding the seedy character of the confidential informer. They both speak well, without hemming and hawing, without stum-bling over syntactic cliffs, better than senators at a press con-ference. Thus, like rival suitors, they begin to woo the jury.

At mid-morning, before hearing from the first witness, we take a recess. (It sounds more and more like school.) Thirteen of us with peel-away JUROR tags stuck to our shirts and sweaters retreat to the jury room. We drink coffee and make polite chat. Since the only thing we have in common is this trial, and since the judge has just forbidden us to talk about that, we grind our gears trying to get a conversation started. I find out what everybody does in the way of work: a bar waitress, a TV repairman (losing customers while he sits here), a department store security guard, a dentist's assistant, an accountant, a nursing home nurse, a cleaning woman, a caterer, a mason, a boisterous old lady retired from rearing children (and married, she tells us, to a school-crossing guard), a meek college student with the demeanor of a groundhog, a teacher. Three of them right now are unemployed. Six men, six women, with ages ranging from twenty-one to somewhere above seventy. Chaucer could gather this bunch together for a literary pilgrimage, and he would not have a bad sampling of smalltown America.

Presently the bailiff looks in to see what we're up to. She is a jowly woman, fiftyish, with short hair the color and texture of buffed aluminum. She wears silvery half-glasses of the sort favored by librarians; in the courtroom she peers at us above the frames with a librarian's skeptical glance, as if to make sure we are awake. To each of us she now gives a small yellow pad and a ballpoint pen. We are to write our names on the back, take notes on them during the trial, and surrender them to her whenever we leave the courtroom. (School again.) Without saying so directly, she lets us know that we are her flock and she is our shepherd. Anything we need, any yen we get for traveling, we should let her know.

I ask her whether I can go downstairs for a breath of air, and the bailiff answers "sure." On the stairway I pass a teenage boy who is listlessly polishing with a rag the wrought-iron filigree that supports the banister. Old men sheltering from December slouch on benches just inside the ground-floor entrance of the courthouse. Their faces have been caved in by disappointment and the loss of teeth. Two-dollar cotton work gloves, the cheapest winter hand-covers, stick out of their back pockets. They are veterans of this place; so when they see me coming with the blue JUROR label pasted on my chest, they look away. Don't tamper with jurors, especially under the very nose of the law. I want to tell them I'm not a real juror, only a spare, number thirteen. I want to pry old stories out of them, gossip about hunting and dogs, about their favorite pickup trucks, their worst jobs. I want to ask them when and how it all started to go wrong for them. Did they hear a snap when the seams of their life began to come apart? But they will not be fooled into looking at me, not these wily old men with the crumpled faces. They believe the label on my chest and stare down at their unlaced shoes.

I stick my head out the door and swallow some air. The lighted thermometer on the bank reads twenty-eight degrees. Schmaltzy Christmas organ music rebounds from the brick-and-limestone shopfronts of the town square. The Salvation Army bell rings and rings. Delivery trucks hustling through yellow lights blare their horns at jaywalkers.

The bailiff must finally come fetch me, and I feel like a wayward sheep. On my way back upstairs, I notice the boy dusting the same square foot of iron filigree, and realize that he is doing this as a penance. Some judge ordered him to clean the metalwork. I'd like to ask the kid what mischief he's done, but the bailiff, looking very dour, is at my heels.

In the hallway she lines us up in our proper order, me last. Everybody stands up when we enter the courtroom, and then, as if we have rehearsed these routines, we all sit down at once. Now come the facts.

The facts are a mess. They are full of gaps, chuckholes, switchbacks, and dead ends—just like life.

At the outset we are shown three small plastic bags. Inside the first is a wad of aluminum foil about the size of an earlobe; the second contains two white pills; the third holds a pair of stamp-sized, squarish packets of folded brown paper. A chemist from the state police lab testifies that he examined these items and found cocaine inside the brown packets, hashish inside the wad of aluminum foil. As for the white pills, they are counterfeits of a popular barbiturate, one favored by politicians and movie stars. They're depressants—downers—but they contain no "controlled substances."

There follows half a day's worth of testimony about how the bags were sealed, who locked them in the narcotics safe at the Bloomington police station, which officer drove them up to the lab in Indianapolis and which drove them back again, who carried them in his coat pocket and who carried them in his briefcase. Even the judge grows bored during this tedious business. He yawns, tips back in his chair, sips coffee from a mug, folds and unfolds with deft thumbs a square of paper about the size of the cocaine packets. The wheels of justice grind slowly. We hear from police officers in uniform, their handcuffs clanking, and from mustachioed officers in civvies, revolvers bulging under their suitcoats. From across the courtroom, the bailiff glares at us above her librarian's glasses, alert to catch us napping. She must be an expert at judging the degrees of tedium.

"Do you have to go back and be in the jail again tomorrow?" my little boy asks me at supper.

"Not jail," I correct him. "*Jury.* I'm in the jury."

"With real police?"

"Yes."

"And guns?"

"Yes, real guns."

On the second day there is much shifting of limbs in the jury box when the confidential informer, whom the police call I90, takes the stand. Curly-haired, thirty-three years old, bear-built and muscular like a middle-range wrestler, slow of eye, calm under the crossfire of questions, I90 works—when he works—as a dry-wall finisher. (In other words, he gets plasterboard ready for painting. It's a dusty, blinding job; you go home powdered white as a ghost, and you taste the joint-filler all night.) Like roughly one-quarter of the construction workers in the county, right now he's unemployed.

The story he tells is essentially this: Just under a year ago, two cops showed up at his house. They'd been tipped off that he had a mess of stolen goods in his basement, stuff he'd swiped from over in a neighboring county. "Now look here," the cops said to him, "you help us out with some cases we've got going, and we'll see what we can do to help you when this here burglary business comes to court." "Like how?" he said. "Like tell us what you know about hot property, and maybe finger a drug dealer or so." He said yes to that, with the two cops sitting at his kitchen table, and—zap!—he was transformed into I90. (Hearing of this miraculous conversion, I am reminded of Saul on the road to Damascus, the devil's agent suddenly seeing the light and joining the angels.) In this new guise he gave information that led to several arrests and some prison terms, including one for his cousin and two or three for other buddies.

In this particular case, his story goes on, he asked a good friend of his where a guy could buy some, you know, drugs. The friend's brother led him to Bennie's trailer, where Bennie offered to sell I90 about any kind of drug a man's heart could desire. "All I want's some hash," I90 told him, "but I got to go get some money off my old lady first." "Then go get it," said Bennie.

Where I90 went was to the police station. There they fixed him up to make a "controlled buy": searched him, searched his car; strapped a radio transmitter around his waist; took his money and gave him twenty police dollars to make the deal. Back I90 drove to Bennie's place, and on his tail in an unmarked police car drove Officer B., listening over the radio to every burp and glitch sent out by I90's secret transmitter. On the way, I90 picked up a six-pack of Budweiser. ("If you walk into a suspect's house drinking a can of beer," Officer B. later tells us, "usually nobody'll guess you're working for the police.") Inside the trailer, the woman Bennie lives with was now fixing supper, and her three young daughters were playing cards on the linoleum floor. I90 bought a gram of blond Lebanese hashish from Bennie for six dollars. Then I90 said that his old lady was on him bad to get her some downers, and Bennie obliged by selling him a couple of 714's (the white pills favored by movie stars and politicians) at seven dollars for the pair. They shot the bull awhile, Bennie bragging about

141

how big a dealer he used to be (ten pounds of hash and five hundred hits of acid a week), I90 jawing along like an old customer. After about twenty minutes in the trailer, I90 drove to a secluded spot near the L & N railroad depot, and there he handed over the hash and pills to Officer B., who milked the details out of him.

Four days later, I90 went through the same routine, this time buying two packets of cocaine—two "dimes'" worth—from Bennie for twenty dollars. Inside the trailer were half a dozen or so of Bennie's friends, drinking whiskey and smoking pot and watching TV and playing backgammon and generally getting the most out of a Friday night. Again Officer B. tailed I90, listened to the secret radio transmission, and took it all down in a debriefing afterwards behind the Colonial Bakery.

The lawyers burn up a full day leading I90 through this story, dropping questions like breadcrumbs to lure him on, Mr. Prosecutor trying to guide him out of the labyrinth of memory and Mr. Defense trying to get him lost. I90 refuses to get lost. He tells and retells his story without stumbling, intent as a wrestler on a dangerous hold.

On the radio news I hear that U.S. ships have intercepted freighters bound out from Beirut carrying tons and tons of Lebanese hashish, the very same prize strain of hash that I90 claims he bought from Bennie. Not wanting to irk the Lebanese government, the radio says, our ships let the freighters through. Tons and tons sailing across the Mediterranean—into how many one-gram slugs could that cargo be divided?

Out of jail the defense lawyers subpoena one of I90's brothers, who is awaiting his own trial on felony charges. He has a rabbity look about him, face pinched with fear, ready to bolt for the nearest exit. His canary yellow T-shirt is emblazoned with a scarlet silhouette of the Golden Gate Bridge. The shirt and the fear make looking at him painful. He is one of seven brothers and four

142

sisters. Hearing that total of eleven children—the same number as in my father's family—I wonder if the parents were ever booked for burglary or other gestures of despair.

This skittish gent tells us that he always buys his drugs from his brother, good old I90. And good old I90, he tells us further, has a special fondness for snorting cocaine. Glowing there on the witness stand in his yellow shirt, dear brother gives the lie to one after another of I90's claims. But just when I'm about ready, hearing all of this fraternal gossip, to consign I90 to the level of hell reserved by Dante for liars, the prosecutor takes over the questioning. He soon draws out a confession that there has been a bitter feud recently between the two brothers. "And haven't you been found on three occasions to be mentally incompetent to stand trial?" the prosecutor demands.

"Yessir," mutters the brother.

"And haven't you spent most of the past year in and out of mental institutions?"

"Yessir."

This second admission is so faint, like a wheeze, that I must lean forward to hear it, even though I am less than two yards away. While the prosecutor lets this damning confession sink into the jury, the rabbity brother just sits there, as if exposed on a rock while the hawks dive, his eyes pinched closed.

By day three of the trial, we jurors are no longer strangers to one another. Awaiting our entry into court, we exhibit wallet photos of our children, of nieces and nephews. We moan in chorus about our Christmas shopping lists. The caterer tells about serving 3,000 people at a basketball banquet. The boisterous old lady, to whom we have all taken a liking, explains how the long hairs on her white cats used to get on her husband's black suit pants until she put the cats out in the garage with heating pads in their boxes.

"Where do you leave your car?" the accountant asks.

"On the street," explains the lady. "I don't want to crowd those cats. They're particular as all get-out."

People compare their bowling scores, their insurance rates, their diets. The mason, who now weighs about 300 pounds, recounts how he once lost 129 pounds in nine months. His blood pressure got so bad he had to give up dieting, and inside of a year he'd gained all his weight back and then some. The nurse, who wrestles the bloated or shriveled bodies of elderly paupers at the city's old folks' home, complains about her leg joints, and we all sympathize. The security guard entertains us with sagas about shoplifters. We compare notes on car wrecks, on where to get a transmission overhauled, on the outgoing college football coach and the incoming city mayor. We talk, in fact, about everything under the sun except the trial.

In the hall, where we line up for our reentry into the courtroom, a sullen boy sits at a table scrawling on a legal pad. Line after line he copies the same sentence: "I never will steal anything ever again." More penance. He's balancing on the first rung of a ladder that leads up—or down—to the electric chair. Somewhere in the middle of the ladder is a good long prison sentence, and that, I calculate, is what is at stake in our little drug-dealing case.

On the third day of testimony, we learn that 190 has been hidden away overnight by police. After he stepped down from the witness stand yesterday, Bennie's mate, Rebecca, greeted the informant outside in the lobby and threatened to pull a bread knife out of her purse and carve him into mincemeat. I look with new interest at the stolid, bulky, black-haired woman who has been sitting since the beginning of the trial right behind the defendant. From time to time she has leaned forward, touched Bennie on the shoulder, and bent close to whisper something in his good ear. She reminds me of the Amish farm wives of my Ohio childhood—stern, unpainted, built stoutly for heavy chores, her face a fortress against outsiders.

144

When Rebecca takes the stand, just half a dozen feet from where I sit in chair thirteen, I sense a tigerish fierceness beneath her numb surface. She plods along behind the prosecutor's questions until he asks her, rhetorically, whether she would like to see Bennie X put in jail; then she lashes out. God no, she doesn't want him locked away. Didn't he take her in when she had two kids already and a third in the oven, and her first husband run off, and the cupboards empty? And haven't they been living together just as good as married for eight years, except while he was in jail, and don't her three little girls call him Daddy? And hasn't he been working on the city garbage trucks, getting up at four in the morning, coming home smelling like other people's trash, and hasn't she been bagging groceries at the supermarket, her hands slashed with paper cuts, and her mother looking after the girls, all so they can keep off the welfare? Damn right she doesn't want him going to any prison.

What's more, Rebecca declares, Bennie don't deserve prison because he's clean. Ever since he got out of the slammer a year ago, he's quit dealing. He's done his time and he's mended his ways and he's gone straight. What about that sale of cocaine? the prosecutor wants to know. It never happened, Rebecca vows. She was there in the trailer the whole blessed night, and she never saw Bennie sell nobody nothing, least of all cocaine, which he never used because it's too expensive—it'll run you seventy-five dollars a day—and which he never sold even when he was dealing. The prosecutor needles her: How can she remember that particular night so confidently? She can remember, she flares at him, because early that evening she got a call saying her sister's ten-year-old crippled boy was fixing to die, and all the family was going to the children's hospital in Indianapolis to watch him pass away. That was a night she'll never forget as long as she lives.

When I was a boy, my friends and I believed that if you killed a snake, the mate would hunt you out in your very bed and strangle or gnaw or smother you. We held a similar belief regarding

145

bears, wolves, and mountain lions, although we were much less likely to run into any of those particular beasts. I have gone years without remembering that bit of child's lore, until today, when Rebecca's tigerish turn on the witness stand revives it. I can well imagine her stashing a bread knife in her purse. And if she loses her man for years and stony years, and has to rear those three girls alone, the cupboards empty again, she might well jerk that knife out of her purse one night and use it on something other than bread.

During recess, we thirteen sit in the jury room and pointedly avoid talking about the bread knife. The mason tells how a neighbor kid's Ford Pinto skidded across his lawn and onto his front porch, blocking the door and nosing against the picture window. "I took the wheels off and chained the bumper to my maple tree until his daddy paid for fixing my porch."

Everyone, it seems, has been assaulted by a car or truck. Our vehicular yarns wind closer and closer about the courthouse. Finally, two of the women jurors—the cigarillo-smoking caterer and the elderly cat lady—laugh nervously. The two of them were standing just inside the plate-glass door of the courthouse last night, the caterer says, when along came a pickup truck, out poked an arm from the window, up flew a smoking beer can, and then BAM! the can exploded. "We jumped a yard in the air!" cries the old woman. "We thought it was some of Bennie's mean-looking friends," the caterer admits. Everybody laughs at the tableau of speeding truck, smoking can, exploding cherry bomb, leaping jurors. Then we choke into sudden silence, as if someone has grabbed each of us by the throat.

Four of Bennie's friends—looking not so much mean as broken, like shell-shocked refugees—testify on his behalf during the afternoon of day three. Two of them are out-of-work men in their twenties, with greasy hair to their shoulders, fatigue jackets, and clodhopper boots: their outfits and world-weary expressions are

146

borrowed from record jackets. They are younger versions of the old men with caved-in faces who crouch on benches downstairs, sheltering from December. The other two witnesses are young women with reputations to keep up, neater than the scruffy men; gold crosses dangle over their sweaters, and gum cracks between crooked teeth. All four speak in muttered monosyllables and orphaned phrases, as if they are breaking a long vow of silence and must fetch bits and pieces of language from the archives of memory. They were all at Bennie's place on the night of the alleged cocaine sale, and they swear in unison that no such sale took place.

Officer B., the puppetmaster who pulled the strings on 190, swears just as adamantly that both the sales, of cocaine and of hash, *did* take place, for he listened to the proceedings over the radio in his unmarked blue Buick. He is a sleepy-eyed man in his mid-thirties, about the age of the informant and the defendant, a law-upholding alter ego for those skewed souls.

Double-chinned, padded with the considerable paunch that seems to be issued along with the police badge, Officer B. answers Mr. Prosecutor and Mr. Defense in a flat, walkie-talkie drawl, consulting a sheaf of notes in his lap, never contradicting himself. Yes, he neglected to tape the opening few minutes of the first buy, the minutes when the exchange of hashish and money actually took place. Why? "I had a suspicion my batteries were weak, and I wanted to hold off." And, yes, he did erase the tape of the debriefing that followed buy number one. Why? "It's policy to reuse the old cassettes. Saves the taxpayers' money." And, yes, the tape of the second buy is raw, indecipherable noise, because a blaring TV in the background drowns out all human voices. (Listening to the tape, we can understand nothing in the scrawking except an ad for the American Express Card.) The tapes, in other words, don't prove a thing. What it all boils down to is the word of the law and of the unsavory informer versus the word of the many-times-convicted defendant, his mate, and his friends.

147

Toward the end of Officer B.'s testimony, there is a resounding clunk, like a muffled explosion, at the base of the witness stand. We all jump—witness, judge, jury, onlookers—and only relax when the prosecutor squats down and discovers that a pair of handcuffs has fallen out of Officer B.'s belt. Just a little reminder of the law's muscle. All of us were envisioning bombs. When Officer B. steps down, the tail of his sportcoat is hitched up over the butt of his gun.

The arrest: A squad car pulls up to the front of the trailer, and out the trailer's back door jumps Bennie, barefooted, wearing T-shirt and cut-off jeans. He dashes away between tarpaper shacks, through dog yards, over a stubbled field (his bare feet bleeding), through a patch of woods to a railroad cut. Behind him puffs a skinny cop (who recounts this scene in court), shouting, "Halt! Police!" But Bennie never slows down until he reaches that railroad cut, where he stumbles, falls, rolls down to the tracks like the sorriest hobo. The officer draws his gun. Bennie lifts his hands for the familiar steel cuffs. The two of them trudge back to the squad car, where Officer B. reads the arrest warrant and Bennie blisters everybody with curses.

The judge later instructs us that flight from arrest may be regarded as evidence, not of guilt but of *consciousness* of guilt. Oh ho! A fine distinction! Guilt for what! Selling drugs? Playing hooky? Original sin? Losing his job at Coca-Cola? I think of those bleeding feet, the sad chase. I remember a drunken uncle who stumbled down a railroad cut, fell asleep between the tracks, and died of fear when a train passed over.

On day four of the trial, Bennie himself takes the stand. He is shorter than I thought, and fatter—too many months of starchy jail food and no exercise. With exceedingly long thumbnails he scratches his jaw. When asked a question, he rolls his eyes, stares at the ceiling, then answers in a gravelly country voice, the voice

148

of a late-night disk jockey. At first he is gruffly polite, brief in his replies, but soon he gets cranked up and rants in a grating monologue about his painful history.

He graduated from high school in 1968, worked eight months at RCA and Coca-Cola, had a good start, had a sweetheart, then the Army got him, made him a cook, shipped him to Vietnam. After a few weeks in the kitchen, he was transferred to the infantry because the fodder-machine was short of foot soldiers. "Hey, listen, man, I ain't nothing but a cook," he told them. "I ain't been trained for combat." And they said, "Don't you worry; you'll get on-the-job training. Learn or die." The artillery ruined his hearing. (Throughout the trial he has held a hand cupped behind one ear, and has followed the proceedings like a grandfather.) Some of his buddies got shot up. He learned to kill people. "We didn't even know what we was there for." To relieve his constant terror, he started doing drugs: marijuana, opium, just about anything that would ease a man's mind. Came home from Vietnam in 1971 a wreck, got treated like dirt, like a babykiller, like a murdering scumbag, and found no jobs. His sweetheart married an insurance salesman.

Within a year after his return he was convicted of shoplifting and burglary. He was framed on the second charge by a friend, but couldn't use his only alibi because he had spent the day of the robbery in bed with a sixteen-year-old girl, whose father would have put him away for statutory rape. As it was, he paid out two years in the pen, where he sank deeper into drugs than ever before. "If you got anything to buy or trade with, you can score more stuff in the state prisons than on the streets of Indianapolis." After prison, he still couldn't find work, couldn't get any help for his drug-thing from the Veterans' Administration, moved in with Rebecca and her three girls, eventually started selling marijuana and LSD. "Everytime I went to somebody for drugs, I got ripped off. That's how I got into dealing. If you're a user, you're always looking for a better deal."

In 1979 he was busted for selling hash, in 1980 for possessing acid, betrayed in both cases by the man from whom he had bought his stock. "He's a snitch, just a filthy snitch. You can't trust nobody." Back to prison for a year, back out again in December 1981. No jobs, no jobs, no damn jobs; then part-time on the city garbage truck, up at four in the morning, minus five degrees and the wind blowing and the streets so cold his gloves stuck to the trash cans. Then March came, and this I90 guy showed up, wanted to buy some drugs, and "I told him I wasn't dealing any more. I done my time and gone straight. I told him he didn't have enough money to pay me for no thirty years in the can." (The prosecutor bristles, the judge leans meaningfully forward: we jurors are not supposed to have any notion of the sentence that might follow a conviction on this drug charge.)

In his disk-jockey voice, Bennie denies ever selling anything to this I90 snitch. (He keeps using the word "snitch": I think of tattle-tales, not this adult betrayal.) It was I90, he swears, who tried to sell *him* the hash. Now the pills, why, those he had lying around for a friend who never picked them up, and so he just gave them to I90. "They was give to me, and so I couldn't charge him nothing. They wasn't for me anyway. Downers I do not use. To me, life is a downer. Just to cope with every day, that is way down low enough for me." And as for the cocaine, he never laid eyes on it until the man produced that little plastic bag in court. "I don't use coke. It's too expensive. That's for the bigwigs and the upstanding citizens, as got the money."

Sure, he admits, he ran when the police showed up at his trailer. "I'm flat scared of cops. I don't like talking to them about anything. Since I got back from Vietnam, every time they cross my path they put bracelets on me." (He holds up his wrists. They are bare now, but earlier this morning, when I saw a deputy escorting him into the courthouse, they were handcuffed.) He refuses to concede that he is a drug addict, but agrees he has a terrible habit, "a gift from my country in exchange for me going overseas and killing a bunch of strangers."

After the arrest, forced to go cold turkey on his dope, he begged the jail doctor—"He's no kind of doctor, just one of them that fixes babies"—to zonk him out on something. And so, until the trial, he has spent eight months drowsing under Valium and Thorazine. "You can look down your nose at me for that if you want, but last month another vet hung himself two cells down from me." (The other guy was a scoutmaster, awaiting trial for sexually molesting one of his boys. He had a record of severe depression dating from the war, and used his belt for the suicide.)

"The problem with my life," says Bennie, "is Vietnam." For awhile after coming home, he slept with a knife under his pillow. Once, wakened suddenly, thinking he was still in Vietnam, he nearly killed his best friend. During the week of our trial, another Vietnam vet up in Indianapolis shot his wife in the head, imagining she was a gook. Neighbors got to him before he could pull out her teeth, as he used to pull out the teeth of the enemies he bagged over in Vietnam.

When I look at Bennie, I see a double image. He was drafted during the same month in which I, studying in England, gave Uncle Sam the slip. I hated that war, and feared it, for exactly the reasons he describes—because it was foul slaughter, shameful, sinful, pointless butchery. While he was over there killing and dodging, sinking into the quicksand of drugs, losing his hearing, storing up a lifetime's worth of nightmares, I was snug in England, filling my head with words. We both came home to America in the same year, I to job and family, he to nothing. Ten years after that homecoming, we stare across the courtroom at one another as into a funhouse mirror.

As the twelve jurors file past me into the room where they will decide on Bennie's guilt or innocence, three of them pat my arm in a comradely way. They withdraw beyond a brass-barred gate; I sit down to wait on a deacon's bench in the hallway outside the courtroom. I feel stymied, as if I have rocketed to the moon only to be left riding the ship round and round in idle orbit while my fellow astronauts descend to the moon's surface. At the same time I feel profoundly relieved, because, after the four days of testimony, I still cannot decide whether Bennie truly sold those drugs, or whether I90, to cut down on his own prison time, set up this ill-starred Bennie for yet another fall. Time, time—it always comes down to time: in jail, job, and jury box we are spending and hoarding our only wealth, the currency of days.

Even through the closed door of the courtroom, I still hear the ticking of the clock. The sound reminds me of listening to my daughter's pulse through a stethoscope when she was still riding, curled up like a stowaway, in my wife's womb. Ask not for whom this heart ticks, whispered my unborn daughter through the stethoscope: it ticks for thee. So does the courtroom clock. It grabs me by the ear and makes me fret about time—about how little there is of it, about how we are forever bumming it from one another as if it were cups of sugar or pints of blood ("You got a minute?" "Sorry, have to run, not a second to spare"). Seize the day, we shout, to cheer ourselves; but the day has seized us and flings us forward pell-mell toward the end of all days.

Now and again there is a burst of laughter from the jury room, but it is always squelched in a hurry. They are tense, and laugh to relieve the tension, and then feel ashamed of their giddiness. Lawyers traipse past me—the men smoking, striking poses, their faces like lollipops atop their ties; the women teetering on high heels. The bailiff walks into our judge's office carrying a bread knife. To slice her lunch? As evidence against Rebecca? A moment later she emerges bearing a piece of cake and licking her fingers. Christmas parties are breaking out all over the courthouse.

Rebecca herself paces back and forth at the far end of my hallway, her steps as regular as the clock's tick, killing time. Her bearded and cross-wearing friends sidle up to comfort her, but she shrugs them away. Once she paces down my way, glances at the barred door of the jury room, hears muffled shouts. This she must take for good news, because she throws me a rueful smile before turning back.

Evidently the other twelve are as muddled by the blurred and contradictory "facts" of the case as I am, for they spend from noon until five reaching their decision. They ask for lunch. They ask for a dictionary. They listen again to the tapes. Sullen teenagers, following in the footsteps of Bennie and I90, slouch into the misdemeanor office across the hall from me; by and by they slouch back out again, looking unrepentant. At length the 300-pound mason lumbers up to the gate of the jury room and calls the bailiff. "We're ready as we're going to be." He looks bone-weary, unhappy, and dignified. Raising his eyebrows at me, he shrugs. Comrades in uncertainty.

The cast reassembles in the courtroom, the judge asks the jury for its decision, and the mason stands up to pronounce Bennie guilty. I stare at my boots. Finally I glance up, not at Bennie or Rebecca or the lawyers, but at my fellow jurors. They look distraught, wrung-out and despairing, as if they have just crawled out of a mine after an explosion and have left some of their buddies behind. Before quitting the jury room, they composed and signed a letter to the judge pleading with him to get some help— drug help, mind help, any help—for Bennie.

The ticking of the clock sounds louder in my ears than the judge's closing recital. But I do, with astonishment, hear him say that we must all come back tomorrow for one last piece of business. He is sorry, he knows we are worn out, but the law has prevented him from warning us ahead of time that we might have to decide on one more question of guilt.

The legal question posed for us on the morning of day five is simple: Has Bennie been convicted, prior to this case, of two or more unrelated felonies? If so, then he is defined by Indiana state law as a "habitual offender," and we must declare him to be such.

153

We are shown affidavits for those earlier convictions—burglary, sale of marijuana, possession of LSD—and so the answer to the legal question is clear.

But the moral and psychological questions are tangled, and they occupy the jury for nearly five more hours on this last day of the trial. Is it fair to sentence a person again, after he has already served time for his earlier offenses? How does the prosecutor decide when to apply the habitual offender statute, and does its use in this case have anything to do with the political ambitions of the sleek young attorney? Did Bennie really steal that $150 stereo, for which he was convicted a decade ago, or did he really spend the day in bed with his sixteen-year-old girlfriend? Did Vietnam poison his mind and blight his life?

Two sheriff's deputies guard the jury today; another guards me in my own little cell. The bailiff would not let me stay out on the deacon's bench in the hall, and so, while a plainclothes detective occupies my old seat, I sit in a room lined with file cabinets and stare out like a prisoner through the glass door. "I have concluded," wrote Pascal, "that the whole misfortune of men comes from a single thing, and that is their inability to remain at rest in a room." I agree with him; nothing but that cruising deputy would keep me here.

This time, when the verdict is announced, Rebecca has her daughters with her, three little girls frightened into unchildlike stillness by the courtroom. Their lank hair and washed-out eyes remind me of my childhood playmates, the children of dead-end, used-up West Virginia coalminers who'd moved to Ohio in search of work. The mother and daughter are surrounded by half a dozen rough customers, guys my age with hair down over their shoulders and rings in their ears, with flannel shirts, unfocused eyes. Doubtless they are the reason so many holstered deputies and upholstered detectives are patrolling the courthouse, and the reason I was locked safely away in a cell while the jury deliberated.

154

When the mason stands to pronounce another verdict of guilty, I glimpse what I do not want to glimpse: Bennie flinging his head back, Rebecca snapping hers forward into her palms, the girls wailing.

The judge accompanies all thirteen of us into the jury room, where he keeps us for an hour while the deputies clear the rough customers from the courthouse. We are not to be alarmed, he reassures us; he is simply being cautious, since so much was at stake for the defendant. "How much?" the mason asks. "Up to twenty-four years for the drug convictions, plus a mandatory thirty years for the habitual offender charges," the judge replies. The cleaning woman, the nurse, and the TV repairman begin crying. I swallow carefully. For whatever it's worth, the judge declares comfortingly, he agrees with our decisions. If we knew as much about this Bennie as he knows, we would not be troubled. And that is just the splinter in the brain, the fact that we know so little—about Bennie, about Vietnam, about drugs, about ourselves—and yet we must grope along in our ignorance, pronouncing people guilty or innocent, squeezing out of one another that precious fluid, time.

And so I do my five days in the thirteenth chair. Bennie may do as many as fifty-four years in prison, buying his drugs from meaner dealers, dreaming of land mines and of his adopted girls, checking the date on his watch, wondering at what precise moment the hinges of his future slammed shut.

Printed in the United States
125613LV00004B/58/A

9 780807 063439